TAKS Mathematics Preparation

Grade 9

Student Edition

A Region IV ESC Resource
Region IV Education Service Center
Houston, Texas

ABOUT THE REGION IV EDUCATION SERVICE CENTER

The Region IV Education Service Center (ESC) supports student achievement by providing educational products and services that focus on Excellence, Service, and Children. We create and conduct professional development institutes, produce research-based instructional materials, and provide technical assistance to strengthen educational systems to promote the academic success of all students.

TAKS Mathematics Preparation Grade 9
Student Edition
Copyright © 2004
Region IV Education Service Center
7145 West Tidwell
Houston, Texas 77092-2096

First Printing, January 2004

ISBN 1-932524-59-2

Additional Products and Services

Please visit our website www.esc4.net to view other products and services provided by Region IV ESC.

Bill McKinney, Ph.D. Executive Director • Region IV ESC is an equal opportunity employer.

Functions

Sugar Free Soda	Plain Soda	Caffeine Free Soda	Code
a1	a2	a3	
Vanilla Soda	Cherry Soda	Grape Juice	
b1	b2	b3	
Apple juice	Orange Juice	Bottled Water	
c1	c2	c3	
Bottled Water			
d1			

a   1
b   2
c   3
d

1. Why would the vending machine company consider the code the independent variable in this situation?

2. Why would the vending machine company consider the drink the dependent variable in this situation?

3. List the elements in the input (domain).

4. List the elements in the output (range).

5. What would be the output for this statement, d(c2)= ?

6. Write the relationship between the orange juice and its code using function notation.

7. If a person enters a code and receives caffeine free soda, what code did they enter?

8. Does this mapping represent a function? Why or why not?

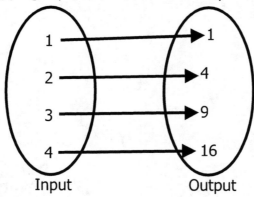

9. If $f(2) = 4$, write the relationship between 4 and 16 in function notation.

10. Does this mapping represent a function? Why or why not?

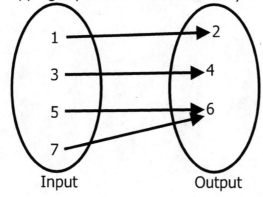

11. Does this mapping represent a function? Why or why not?

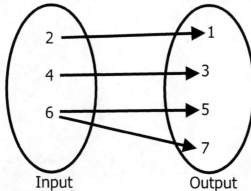

Use the scatterplot below to answer the following questions.

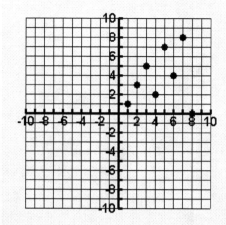

12. Does this scatterplot represent a function? Why or why not?

13. What are the inputs (domain) for this scatterplot?

14. What are the outputs (range) for this scatterplot?

Use the scatterplot below to answer the following questions.

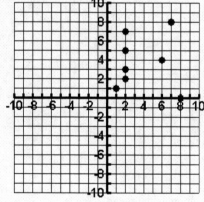

15. Does this scatterplot represent a function? Why or why not?

16. What are the inputs (domain) for this scatterplot?

17. What are the outputs (range) for this scatterplot?

a.   YES   NO   Student arrives at a correct solution?

	4	3	2	1
b. Conceptual Knowledge				
c. Procedural Knowledge				
d. Communication				

The table below shows the relationship between the amount of hours Billy works and the amount of his paycheck. Identify the independent and dependent quantities and justify your answer.

Hours	10	15	20	25
Amount	70	105	140	175

Patterns A

Term Number	Picture	Process	Total Number of Blocks
1			2
2			4
3			6
4			
5			
10			
15			

TAKS Mathematics Preparation Book: Grade 9

Patterns B

Term Number	Picture	Process	Total Number of Blocks
1			4
2			7
3			10
4			
5			
10			
15			

1. Build the first five terms. What patterns do you observe?

2. What are the independent and dependent variables in this situation?

3. What is the rate of change in this situation?

4. Relate the independent and dependent variables to each other in the process column using words, numbers or pictures.

5. Write a relationship sentence (words) that describes the relationship between the independent and dependent variables.

6. Write a function rule for this situation.

7. Enter the data into your graphing calculator and plot that data. How are these data like the data in the **Patterns A** activity page? How are they different?

8. Enter your function rule into your graphing calculator and plot your rule over your data. Is the rule a good fit? Why or why not?

9. What is different about the function rule in this activity and the rule in **Patterns A**? How are they alike?

10. What does the y-intercept (the place where the model crosses the y-axis) represent in the concrete model?

11. How many total blocks would you need to build the thirty-first term? How can you be sure your answer is reasonable?

12. If you built a structure following this pattern using 1127 blocks what term would it be? How can you be sure your answer is reasonable?

Patterns C

Term Number	Picture	Process	Total Number of Blocks
1			3
2			8
3			15
4			
5			
10			
15			

1. Build the first five terms. What patterns do you observe?

2. What are the independent and dependent variables in this situation?

3. What is the rate of change in this situation?

4. Relate the independent and dependent variables to each other in the process column using words, numbers, or pictures.

5. Write a relationship sentence (words) that describes the relationship between the independent and dependent variables.

6. Write a function rule for this situation.

7. Enter the data into your graphing calculator and plot that data. How are these data like the data in the **Patterns A** activity page? How are they different?

8. Enter your function rule into your graphing calculator and plot it over your data. Is the rule a good fit? Why or why not?

9. What is different about the function rule in this activity and the rule in **Patterns A**?

10. How many total blocks would you need to build the fifteenth term? How can you be sure your answer is reasonable?

11. If you built a structure following this pattern using 968 blocks, what term would it be? How can you be sure your answer is reasonable?

a.   YES   NO   Student arrives at a correct solution?

	4	3	2	1
b. Conceptual Knowledge				
c. Procedural Knowledge				
d. Communication				

The graph shows how much gasoline will be left in the gas tank of the Rincon's family car based on the number of miles they drive. A full tank holds 32 gallons. They are planning a trip that is approximately 1310 miles and are thinking that 2 tanks of gas will be sufficient. Are they correct? Justify your answer.

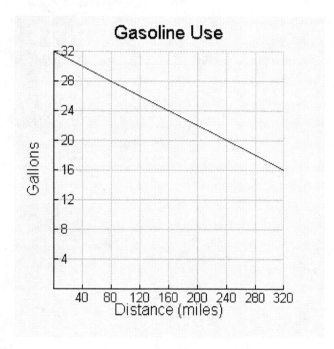

1. A swordfish travels through the water at a speed of 40 miles per hour. The relationship between the distance traveled, d, and the time traveled, t, is determined by the function $d = 40t$. Which of the following statements is true?

    A. The distance a swordfish travels is determined by the size of the swordfish.

    B. The amount of time a swordfish travels is determined by the size of the swordfish.

    C. The amount of time a swordfish travels is determined by the distance the swordfish travels.

    D. The distance a swordfish travels is determined by the amount of time the swordfish travels.

2. Which of the following does not represent a function?

    A.

x	-2	0	4	10
y	-1	3	11	23

    B. $y = x^2 - 3$

    C. $\{(6, -1), (6, 0), (6, 3), (6, 5)\}$

    D.

    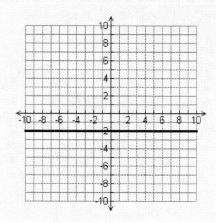

3. Antonio is raising a steer for the county livestock show. The steer was 6 months old and weighed 500 pounds when Antonio bought him. The steer is gaining an average of 65 pounds per month. Which equation describes the relationship between the weight of the steer, w, and the number of months, m, Antonio has owned the steer?

A. $w = 65m$

B. $w = 500 + 65$

C. $w = 500m + 65$

D. $w = 500 + 65m$

4. Carly was looking at the following table of data.

x	y
-3	-12
-1	-8
0	-6
1	-4
3	0

Which of the following statements is true about the data?

A. The rate of change is negative.

B. The y-intercept is 3.

C. The x-intercept is –6.

D. The ordered pair (-2, -10) would also be a data point in the table.

5. Which of the following represents all the solutions to the inequality $2x + 3y \geq -6$?

A.

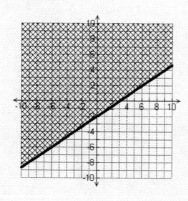

C.

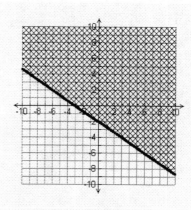

B.

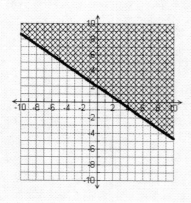

D.

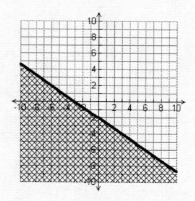

Stretch Data Sheet

Team duties:
Rubber band operator
Meter stick holder
Spotter
Recorder

Procedure:

1. Shoot the rubber band for each stretch amount three times. Observe and record the flight distance for each trial.

2. Calculate the average flight distance for each stretch amount.

Stretch Amount (cm)	Flight Distance (cm)			
	Trial 1	Trial 2	Trial 3	Average
0				
1				
2				
3				
4				
5				
6				

3. Plot the average flight distance vs. stretch.

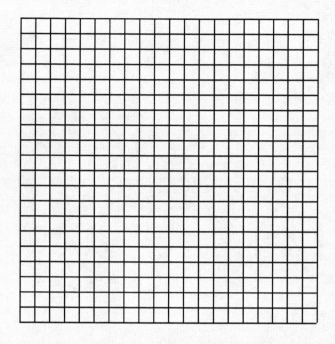

4. Determine a function rule that relates the flight distance to the stretch.

5. Describe a reasonable domain and range for this situation.

6. Based on your model, if a rubber band were stretched 8 centimeters, what would be the approximate flight distance? Justify your answer.

7. Based on your model, if a rubber band had a flight distance of 248 centimeters, approximately how many centimeters was it stretched?

TAKS Mathematics Preparation Book: Grade 9

Paperclip Skydiving

Team duties:
   Timer – times the drops
   Dropper – drops action figure consistently from the designated heights during data collection and during final parachute drop
   Spotter – determines the appropriate drop height during data collection
   Recorder – makes measurements and records data

Procedure:

1. Build a parachute by attaching a paperclip to the handles of the plastic grocery bag.

2. Drop the parachute from the designated heights in the data table. Record the time it takes the parachute to reach the ground.

3. Repeat 3 times. Find the mean time of the three drops and record that number in your data table.

4. Repeat steps 2 and 3 for each height.

Drop Height (cm)	Time of fall (sec)			
	Trial 1	Trial 2	Trial 3	Average
50				
75				
100				
125				
150				
175				
200				

5. Enter your data (Drop height, Average time) into the graphing calculator. Determine an appropriate window and plot your data. Sketch your plot here.

6. Determine a trend line for your data without using regression. Record it here and enter it in your calculator.

7. Use your trend line or your table to predict the number of rubber bands needed for the action figure to bungee from the final location. The goal is to come as close to the floor as possible without hitting. Record that number here.

a.   YES   NO   Student arrives at a correct solution?

	4	3	2	1
b. Conceptual Knowledge				
c. Procedural Knowledge				
d. Communication				

Nick noticed that the goldfish in his outdoor pond are less active when the temperature gets cooler. He checked his fish book and found a table. Nick decided to determine if there is a functional relationship between the respiration rate of goldfish and the temperature of the water. Before he could analyze the data, his younger brother tore the page into little pieces and mixed up his data. From the torn pieces of paper Nick created the following table.

Temperature of Water (°C)	Goldfish Respiration per Minute
24	144
26	154
29	169
22	134
27	159
23	139
30	174
25	149
28	164

Based upon his data, predict the respiration rate of a goldfish when the water temperature is 15°C. Justify your answer.

a.   YES   NO   Student arrives at a correct solution?

		4	3	2	1
b.	Conceptual Knowledge				
c.	Procedural Knowledge				
d.	Communication				

Mr. Smith is considering changing his Internet provider. He is considering two different options. At-Your-Service OnLine charges $47.95 per month with unlimited usage. Eazee OnLine charges $39.99 per month plus $0.20 per hour. For how many hours would he pay the same monthly charge regardless of the Internet provider he chooses? Which provider offers the better deal? Justify your answer.

a.	YES	NO	Student arrives at a correct solution?			
			4	3	2	1
b.	Conceptual Knowledge					
c.	Procedural Knowledge					
d.	Communication					

Josie wants to build a rectangular box to plant a miniature rose bush. The box must be large enough to hold 400 in^3 of potting soil. The length of the box should be three times as long as the height, and the width should be 3 inches wider than the height. The box will not need a lid. Josie finishes her project and calculates the surface area to be 236 in^2. Will the box hold the necessary potting soil? Justify your answer.

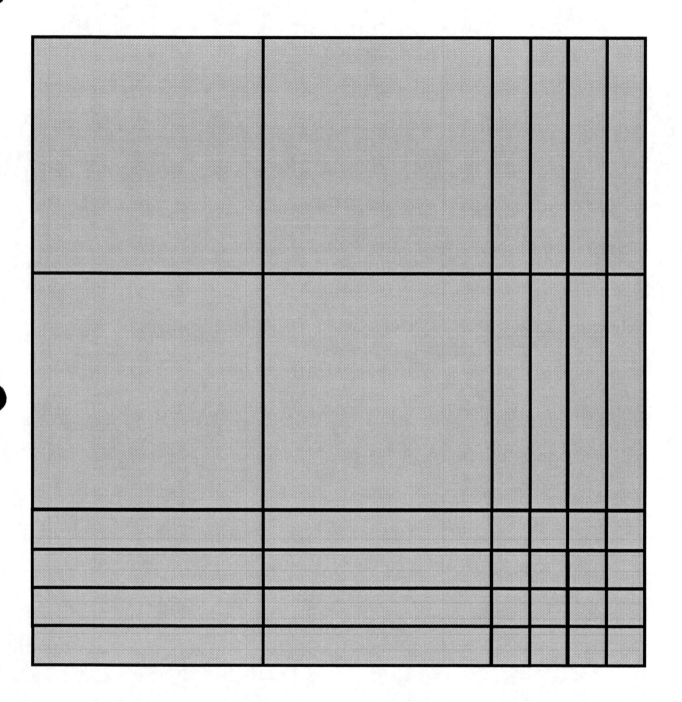

1. Marsha wants to make a scatter plot on her graphing calculator. The data she wants to graph is listed in the table below.

x	y
2	35
4	55
10	115
15	165

If Marsha wants to see all of the ordered pairs, what is the best window setting to use for the domain?

A. x min = -10
    x max = 10

B. x min = -1
    x max = 20

C. y min = -10
    y max = 10

D. y min = 30
    y max = 170

2. Joel is driving from his house in San Antonio. The graph below describes the trip.

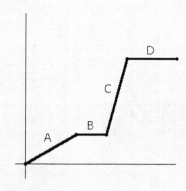

Which portion of the graph represents the period in which Joel was traveling the fastest?

A. A

B. B

C. C

D. D

3. Which table of data below represents a positive correlation between the two variables?

A.

x	y
0	7
1	5
2	3
3	1

C.

x	y
-5	9
-3	5
-2	3
-1	1

B.

x	y
-3	-8
-2	-5
0	1
1	4

D.

x	y
7	0
5	2
3	4
0	7

TAKS Mathematics Preparation Book: Grade 9

4. Emily was factoring a polynomial using tiles. When she finished arranging the tiles the model looked like the picture below.

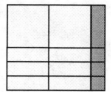

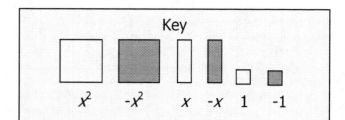

What are the factors of the polynomial?

A. $(2x + 3)(2x - 1)$

B. $(x + 3)(2x + 1)$

C. $(x + 3)(2x - 1)$

D. $(x - 3)(2x + 1)$

5. Kendra wanted to graph the following equation in her graphing calculator.

$$2x - y = 5$$

Which of the following equations should she use?

A. $y = -2x - 5$

B. $y = 3x$

C. $y = -2x + 5$

D. $y = 2x - 5$

Activity Sheet A

Part I: For each of the following, supply the missing information.

The table below shows the amount of money James earns for mowing lawns.

# of hours	Process	James earnings
2		50
3		75
4		100

1. What does the ordered pair (2, 50) mean?

2. Since James works 2 hours and earns $50 and works 3 hours and earns $75, how much does he earn per hour?

3. What is the rate of change for James' job?

4. Write the equation that describes the relationship between the number of hours James works and the amount he earns.

5. Graph the ordered pairs from the table above.

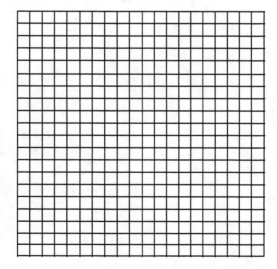

6. What is the vertical change from the ordered pair (2, 50) to the ordered pair (3, 75)?

7. What is the horizontal change from the ordered pair (2, 50) to the ordered pair (3, 75)?

8. Draw a line to connect the points on the graph. Extend the line beyond the points.

9. The amount of slope of the line is the $\dfrac{\text{Vertical Change}}{\text{Horizontal Change}}$ or $\dfrac{\text{Change in y values}}{\text{Change in x values}}$. What is the slope of the line?

10. What is the vertical change from the ordered pair (3, 75) to the ordered pair (4, 100)?

11. What is the horizontal change from the ordered pair (3, 75) to the ordered pair (4, 100)?

12. What is the slope of the line?

Part II: For problems 13 – 18, identify the rate of change or slope.

13. A moving company charges a $20 truck fee and $18 an hour for moving furniture.

14.   rate of change or slope _____

x	Process	y
5		12.50
10		20.00
15		27.50
x		

15.   rate of change or slope _____

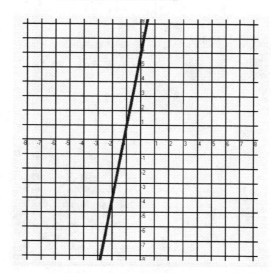

16.   Michele has $150 in the bank. She spends an average of $15 a month.

17.   rate of change or slope _____

x	Process	y
4		1
8		-1
12		-3
x		

18. rate of change or slope _____

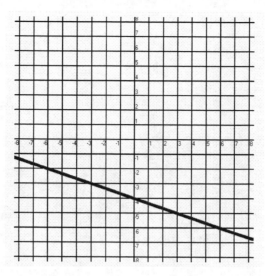

For Problems 19 –21, a rate of change or slope is given. Supply the required information.

19. The rate of change or slope is –16. Create a verbal description that contains this rate/slope.

20. The rate of change or slope is 18. Create a table that contains this rate/slope.

21. The rate of change or slope is 5. Create a graph and equation that contains this rate/slope.

Activity Sheet B

Part I: For problems 1 – 8, identify the rate of change or slope.

1. A lake is 24 feet deep. Each month of the summer the level of water in the lake decreases by $\frac{1}{2}$ a foot.

2. rate of change or slope _____

x	Process	y
4		63
6		87
9		123

3. rate of change or slope _____

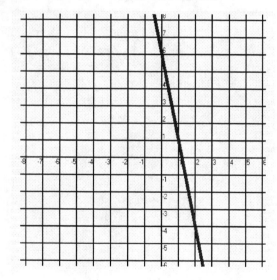

4. $y = 30x + 25$

5. A caterer charges a $20 set up fee plus $7 per person to cater a party.

TAKS Mathematics Preparation Book: Grade 9

6.   rate of change or slope _____

x	Process	y
12		18
17		14
22		10
27		8

7.   rate of change or slope _____

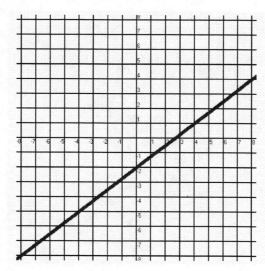

8. $y = 2.75x + 15$

Part II: For problems 9 – 20, supply the required information.
Problems 9 - 10

Olivia	
# of hours	Earnings
2	28
4	39
8	61

Samantha	
# of hours	Earnings
3	31.75
7	60.75
9	75.25

Carolyn	
# of hours	Earnings
5	45
6	50
10	70

9.   Which person earns the most money per hour? How much is the person earning?

10.   Which person earns the least per hour? How much is the person earning?

Problems 11 - 12

Sue	
# of months	Amount remaining
2	180
5	150
7	130

Nancy	
# of months	Amount remaining
4	280
6	270
9	255

Julie	
# of months	Amount remaining
3	88
8	68
10	60

11.   Which person is spending the most per month? How much is the person spending per month?

12.   Which person is spending the least per month? How much is the person spending per month?

Problems 13 - 14

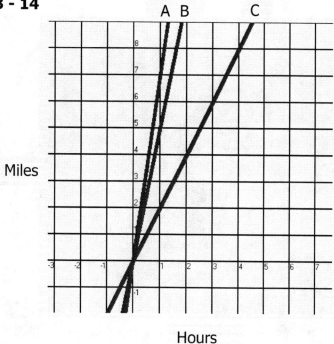

13.   Which graph could represent a person riding a bicycle and traveling at a rate of 5 miles per hour?

14.   Which graph could represent a person riding a bicycle and traveling at a rate of 7 miles an hour?

Problems 15 – 16

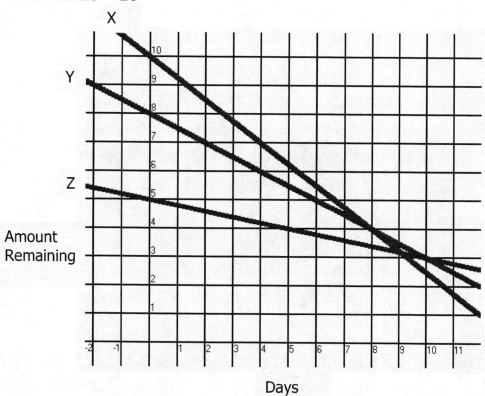

15. Which graph could represent a person spending more than $0.50 a day?

16. Which graph could represent a person spending less than $0.25 a day?

Problems 17 - 18

Patrick's equation of earnings per hour	$y = 15 + 5x$
Scott's equation of earning per hour	$y = 6x + 15$
Michael's equation of earnings per hour	$y = 5x + 10$
Richard's equation of earnings per hour	$y = 5 + 8x$

17. Which two people are earning the same amount of money each hour? How much are they earning per hour?

18. Which person earns the most each hour? How much does the person earn per hour?

Problems 19 – 20

Cindy's equation of spending per month	$y = 200 - 25x$
Martha's equation of spending per month	$y = 200 - 20x$
Julia's equation of spending per month	$y = 275 - 15x$
Angela's equation of spending per month	$y = 150 - 25x$

19. Which two people are spending the same amount of money each month? How much are they spending per month?

20. Which person spends the least amount of money each month? How much is the person spending per month?

a.   YES   NO   Student arrives at a correct solution?

	4	3	2	1
b. Conceptual Knowledge				
c. Procedural Knowledge				
d. Communication				

Mary, Peter, and Paul attended a family reunion in Lubbock this summer. The graph below shows their travel time and distance for this trip. According to the graph, who drove the fastest? Justify your answer.

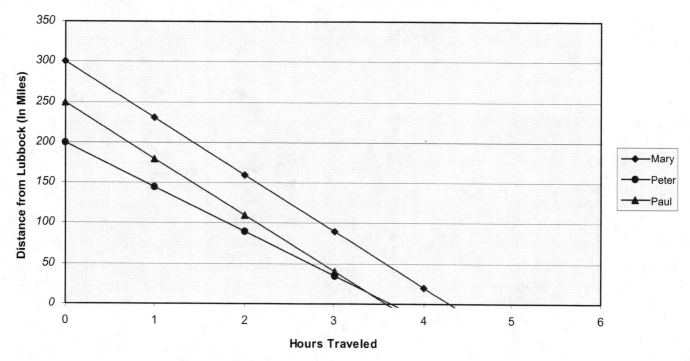

Family Reunion

© 2004 Region IV Education Service Center   TAKS Mathematics Preparation Book: Grade 9

Reproduction authorized only for students of the teacher who purchased this book.

131

Student Name: _____ **Date:** _____

"Examining Equations" Card Match Recording Sheet

1. Find the 6 cards that have equations on them.
2. Sort the remaining cards into 3 groups. You should have a group of cards with a verbal description, a group of cards with a table, and a group of cards with a graph.
3. Match each equation with one card from each of the groups.
4. Record your answers in the spaces provided.
5. You will be assigned one problem to put on chart paper and share with the class.

Equation _____

Verbal description	Table	Graph

Equation _____

Verbal description	Table	Graph

Equation _____

Verbal description	Table	Graph

Equation _____

Verbal description	Table	Graph

Equation _____

Verbal description	Table	Graph

TAKS Mathematics Preparation Book: Grade 9

Student Name: _____ **Date:** _____

Equation _____

Verbal description	Table	Graph

Activity Sheet

1. A mechanic charges a $50 initial fee plus $70 per hour to repair your car. Write an equation that describes the relationship between the number of hours, x, the mechanic works and the amount, y, he charges.

2. A telephone company charges a service fee and a price per minute. The following chart shows the cost of different phone calls.

Number of minutes	Total cost
3	$6.15
5	$6.25
10	$6.50

Write an equation that describes the relationship between the number of minutes, x, and the total cost, y.

3. The table below shows the amount of money Denise earns babysitting.

Number of hours	Earnings
3	$15
5	$25
6	$30

Write an equation that describes the relationship between the number of hours, h, Denise works and the amount she earns, E.

4. Lois weighs 170 pounds. She is losing an average of 3 pounds per week. Write an equation that describes the relationship between Lois' weight, x, and the number of weeks, y, she has been dieting.

5. Diane put an equation in her graphing calculator. This is what her graph looked like. What is the equation of the line she graphed?

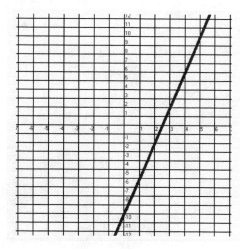

6. Lucy's grandmother gave her $35 for her birthday to start a savings account. Lucy's grandmother also told her that she would give her $5 a month to add to the account. Write and equation to describe the relationship between the amount of money in the account, *y*, and the number of months, *x*, Lucy's grandmother has put money in the account.

For problems 7 – 10, create a table of values and a graph to represent the function.

7. $y = -3x - 2$

x	Process	y

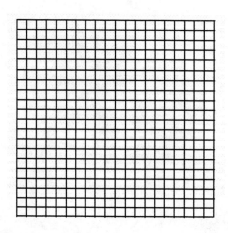

8. $y = 3x + 2$

x	Process	y

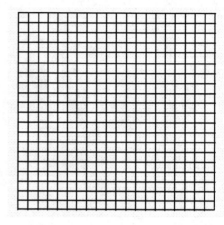

9. $y = \dfrac{1}{3}x - 2$

x	Process	y

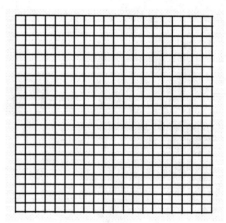

10. $y = -\dfrac{1}{3}x + 2$

x	Process	y

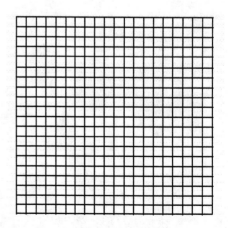

TAKS Mathematics Preparation Book: Grade 9

For problems 11 – 14, write the linear equation that describes each of the following graphs. Then create a verbal description to describe the relationship between the *x*-values and the *y*-values.

11.

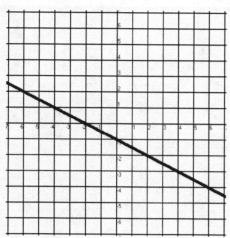

Equation _____

Verbal Description

12.

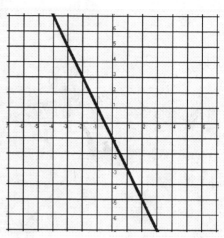

Equation _____

Verbal Description

13.

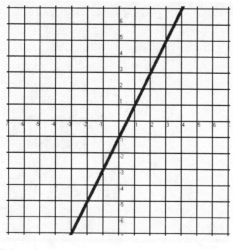

Equation _____

Verbal Description

14.

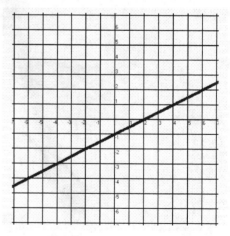

Equation _____

Verbal Description

TAKS Mathematics Preparation Book: Grade 9

a.   YES   NO   Student arrives at a correct solution?

	4	3	2	1
b. Conceptual Knowledge				
c. Procedural Knowledge				
d. Communication				

The Fisher family is taking a camping trip this summer. They plan to canoe down the river. The graph shows how much it will cost to rent a canoe to paddle down the river. If the family rents two canoes for 7 hours each, what will be the cost? Justify your answer.

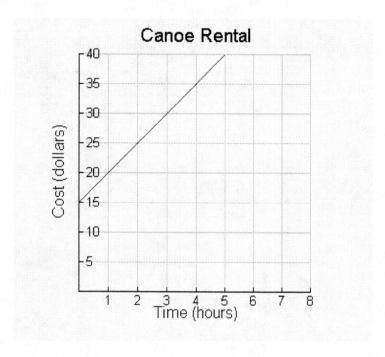

1. Which of the following represents a linear function?

   A. $y = \dfrac{2}{x} + 1$

   B. $y = 2x^2 + 1$

   C. $y = \dfrac{1}{2}x + 1$

   D. $y = x^2$

2. Emily, Josh, Sarah, and Alan were playing a game in which each student was required to draw a card out of a bag. Three of the cards contained information that the student was to use to write the equation of a line while one card had an equation written on it. The cards looked like the ones show below.

Emily's Card	Josh's Card	Sarah's Card	Alan's Card
Slope = 2 y-int. = -3	Slope = 2 Passes through the point (-3, -3)	Passes through the points (0, -3) (2, 1)	$y = 2x - 3$

   After each student finished writing the equation for the information on the card, which student(s) equation would be the same as Alan's equation?

   A. Emily's card only

   B. Josh's card and Sarah's card only

   C. Emily's card and Sarah's card only

   D. Emily's card and Josh's card only

3. Elizabeth graphed a linear function on her graphing calculator. The graph looked like the one below.

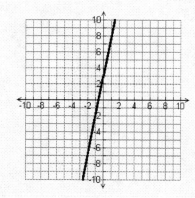

Which of the following would produce a graph exactly like the one Elizabeth graphed?

A.

x	y
-2	13
-1	8
0	3
1	-2

B. $y = 5x - 3$

C. All of the ordered pairs in which the y-coordinate is 5 more than 3 times the x-coordinate.

D. The amount of money, y, in a savings account after x weeks in which a student started with 3 dollars and is saving at a rate of $5 a week.

4. Lucy graphed an equation on her graphing calculator. The graph looked like the graph below.

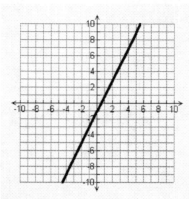

Lucy decided to multiply the slope by –2 and decrease the *y*-intercept by 3 and then graph the new equation. Which of the following graphs looks like Lucy's new graph?

A.

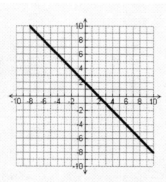

C.

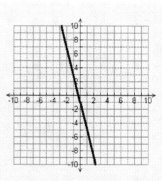

B.

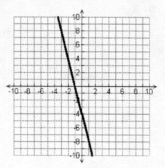

D.

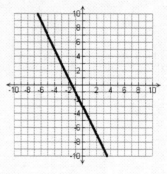

Student Name:_____ **Date:**_____

5. To cater a party, Doris charges an equipment fee plus a food charge per person. She keeps a chart by her telephone so that she can quickly tell a customer how much it will cost to cater a party for x people. The table below is a portion of the chart she created.

# of people (x)	Total cost
25	625
50	1000
75	1375
100	1750

Doris decides she needs to increase the amount she charges her customers. She decides to double the amount she charges per person for food but does not change the equipment fee. After she makes this change in the way she calculates her charges, how much will she charge to cater a party for 75 people?

A. $1625

B. $2500

C. $2750

D. $3750

Braking Distance vs. Speed

The table below lists the speed (in miles per hour) and the braking distance (in feet) for various speeds determined by a researcher. The braking distance is the distance it took the car to stop with good brakes and tires.

Speed (mph)	Braking Distance (ft)
20	35
30	58
40	81
50	104
60	127
70	150

1. Determine a mathematical function between the speed of a car and its braking distance.

2. A person is driving 65 miles per hour, according to the speed limit. Based on your function from number 1, if she steps on the brakes, what would be her braking distance? Use at least three different methods to determine this.

3. A motorcyle magazine once reported the results of stopping a Yamaha motorcycle averaged 87 feet in a series of nine attempts. According to your formula, how fast was the motorcycle going during these tests? Is this a reasonable speed?

Stopping Distance

So far, we have calculated the distance that the car takes to stop once the driver steps on the brake pedal. But how far will the car travel between the time when the driver first perceives the need to stop and when the driver steps on the brakes?

1. To answer this question, you need to consider your reaction time. Imagine you are the driver. From the previous activity, what was your reaction time? What does this time mean?

2. What formula allows you to calculate distance if you know time?

3. What do these variables represent? Which variable is the independent variable? Which variable is the dependent variable? Which variable(s) is/are constant?

   Independent variable:

   Dependent variable:

   Constant(s):

4. On the diagram below, find the place where the car begins stopping. Write the function that describes the relationship between speed and braking distance there. Now, find the place where the driver's reaction time is occurring. Write the distance formula there.

driver needs to stop   driver steps on brakes   car comes to a stop

TAKS Mathematics Preparation Book: Grade 9

5. Keeping in mind the diagram, how could you calculate the stopping distance, or the total distance that it takes for a driver to bring the car to a stop from the moment that he or she first perceives a need to stop?

6. What function models the total stopping distance in terms of the speed of the car?

7. Fill in the stopping distances in the table below using your new function. How do the braking distances and stopping distances compare?

Speed (mph)	Braking Distance (ft)	Stopping Distance (ft)
20	19	
30	43	
40	76	
50	119	
60	171	
70	233	

8. Graph the stopping distance function with the braking distance function using your graphing calculator. Sketch the graphs below. How do the graphs compare?

a.　　YES　　NO　　Student arrives at a correct solution?

	4	3	2	1
b. Conceptual Knowledge				
c. Procedural Knowledge				
d. Communication				

Roderick needs major repairs done on his car. The repair shop gave him an estimate of $2290 to do the repairs. Roderick currently works at a local restaurant and makes $160 a week in wages and tips. He will also earn $35 each weekend by delivering newspapers. If Roderick saves 70% of what he makes, in how many weeks will he have enough money to have the repairs done? Justify your answer.

Activity Sheet A

1. A pet store sells ducks and rabbits. Mr. Rogers bought 5 ducks and 2 rabbits for a total of $112.50. Mrs. McClanahan bought 1 duck and 6 rabbits for a total of $92.50. Let d represent the cost of one duck and r represent the cost of one rabbit.
   a. What equation describes Mr. Rogers' purchase?

   b. What equation describes Mrs. McClanahan's purchase?

   c. What strategy could you use to solve the system?

   d. How much does one duck cost?

   e. How much does one rabbit cost?

2. The perimeter of a rectangle is 48 feet. The width of the rectangle is 4 feet more than three times the length.
   a. What is the formula for the perimeter of a rectangle?

   b. Express the width in terms of length.

   c. What strategy could you use to solve the system?

   d. What is the length of the rectangle?

   e. What is the width of the rectangle?

3. Jaime collects coins. In his collection, there are 57 quarters and dimes that are worth a total of $13.20. Let q represent the number of quarters and d represent the number of dimes.

   a. What equation describes the number of quarters and dimes that Jaime has?

   b. What equation describes the total value of his collection?

   c. What strategy could you use to solve the system?

   d. How many quarters does Jaime have?

   e. How many dimes does Jaime have?

4. A school group with 39 members is going on a summer trip. 9 chaperones will each drive either a van or a car. The vans will hold a total of 6 people, including the driver. The cars will hold 4 people, including the driver. Let v represent the number of vans and c represent the number of cars.

   a. What equation describes the number of vehicles being taken on the trip?

   b. What equation describes the number of people in the vehicles going on the trip?

   c. What strategy could you use to solve the system?

   d. How many cars will be driven?

   e. How many vans will be driven?

a.	YES	NO	Student arrives at a correct solution?			
			4	3	2	1
b.	Conceptual Knowledge					
c.	Procedural Knowledge					
d.	Communication					

Juana is looking for a summer job to earn money for college next year. She finds two job openings through the newspaper. One is for a sales position in the toy department of a local retail store. She would earn $140 per week plus a 20% commission on sales. The second job advertised is for a sales position in an electronics store that would pay $180 per week plus a 10% commission. Juana would prefer to work in the toy department. What would her weekly sales need to be for her to make more money selling toys than selling electronics? Justify your answer.

1. Angela went to a department store and bought a skirt and a blouse. The blouse costs half as much as the skirt. Together the two items cost Angela $39.00. Which equation below could be used to find the cost of the skirt, x?

   A. $\frac{1}{2}x = 39$

   B. $x(\frac{1}{2}x) = 39$

   C. $x + \frac{1}{2}x = 39$

   D. $x + \frac{1}{2} = 39$

2. Which of the following points is located in the solution of $x - 3y \geq 15$?

   A. $(-5, 3)$

   B. $(0, 0)$

   C. $(3, -5)$

   D. $(3, 5)$

TAKS Mathematics Preparation Book: Grade 9

3. Marty has a part-time job mowing lawns. To start his business, Marty spent $325 to buy a lawn mower, a weed eater, and an edger. The gasoline for the equipment costs an average of $4.50 for each yard he mows. Marty decides to charge $30.00 for each yard he mows. Which of the following could Marty use to find the minimum number of yards he must mow, x, before he can make a profit?

I.

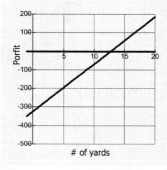

II.

# of yards	Profit
10	-70.00
11	-44.50
12	-19.00
13	6.50
14	32.00

III. $-325 - 4.50x + 30x \leq 0$

A. II only

B. I and II only

C. II and III only

D. I, II, and III

4. Which situation best represents the system of equations shown below?

$$5x + 20y = 55$$
$$x + y = 5$$

I. Allison has 5 bills in her purse. Some of them are five-dollar bills and some of them are twenty-dollar bills. The total value of the bills is $55.00.

II. Mary bought 55 items at the sore. Some of the items cost $5.00 and some of them cost $20.00.

III. There are 5 boxes on a loading dock. Some of the boxes weigh 5 pounds and some of the boxes weigh 20 pounds. The total weight of the boxes is 55 pounds.

A. I only

B. II and III only

C. I and III only

D. I, II, and III

5. Martha has a flower shop. She has 15 pre-made arrangements in her shop. There are twice as many arrangements with roses as there are arrangements with carnations. Which system of equations could be used to determine the number of arrangements with roses, r, and the number of arrangements with carnations, c, that Martha has in her shop?

A. $r + c = 15$
$r = 2c$

B. $r + c = 15$
$c = 2r$

C. $r + 15 = c$
$r = 2c$

D. $c + 15 = r$
$c = 2r$

Activity Sheet A

1. Write $a^4b^7 \times a^2b^3$ without using exponents. DO NOT multiply them out.

    a. How many a's are being multiplied? How many b's are being multiplied?

    b. Rewrite your expression using exponents.

2. Write $m^4n^2 \times m^3n$ without using exponents. DO NOT multiply them out.

    a. How many m's are being multiplied? How many n's are being multiplied?

    b. Rewrite your expression using exponents.

Look at Questions 1 and 2 above. What patterns do you notice?

What rule can you generalize about multiplying expressions with like bases?

Try your new rule:

3. $\left(x^2y^4z^3\right)\left(xy^5z^7\right)$

4. $\left(r^6s^4t^3\right)\left(r^2s^3t^2\right)\left(rs^7t^5\right)$

5. Write $\dfrac{a^4 b^7}{a^2 b^3}$ without using exponents. DO NOT divide them out.

    a. Cancel out any common factors between the numerator and denominator. How many a's remain? How many b's remain?

    b. Rewrite your expression using exponents.

6. Write $\dfrac{m^4 n^5}{m^9 n^2}$ without using exponents. DO NOT divide them out.

    a. Cancel out any common factors between the numerator and denominator. How many m's remain? How many n's remain?

    b. Rewrite your expression using exponents.

Look at Questions 5 and 6 above. What patterns do you notice?

What rule can you generalize about dividing expressions with like bases?

Try your new rule:

7. $\dfrac{x^3 y^4 z^4}{x y^6 z^7}$

8. $\dfrac{r^4 s^3 t^5}{r^4 s^8 t^{10}}$

9. Write $\left(a^3 b^5\right)^2$ without using exponents. DO NOT multiply out.

    a. How many a's are being multiplied? How many b's are being multiplied?

    b. Rewrite your expression using exponents.

10. Write $\left(m^2 n^5\right)^3$ without using exponents. DO NOT multiply out.

    c. How many m's are being multiplied? How many n's are being multiplied?

    d. Rewrite your expression using exponents.

Look at Questions 9 and 10 above. What patterns do you notice?

What rule can you generalize about raising expressions with like bases to a power?

Try your new rule:

11. $\left(x^3 y^4 z^4\right)^2$ 12. $\left(r^4 s^3 t^5\right)^4$

Activity Sheet B

Use your TAKS formula chart to identify the following formulas:

Area of rectangle: Area of trapezoid:

Area of triangle:

1. Calculate the area of a rectangle that has a length of $x^3 y^4 z^6$ and a width of $xy^2 z^2$.

2. Calculate the area of a trapezoid that has base lengths of $s^3 t^5$ and $3s^3 t^5$, and a height of $s^2 t^4$.

3. Calculate the area of a triangle that has a base of $8m^2 n^7$ and a height of $3m^4 n$.

4. If a rectangle has an area of $16x^7 y^4$ and a base of $2x^4 y$, what is its height?

5. If a triangle has an area of $48m^{12} n^{10}$ and a height of $16m^6 n^3$, what is its base?

6. Distance (*d*), rate (*r*), and time (*t*) are related by the formula $d = rt$. If a ball rolls $36p^4 q^9$ feet for $4p^2 q^3$ minutes, what is the speed?

a.	YES	NO	Student arrives at a correct solution?			
			4	3	2	1
b.	Conceptual Knowledge					
c.	Procedural Knowledge					
d.	Communication					

At the Bunny Express rabbit farm, the number of rabbits doubles every month. They began in January with one rabbit, and in February had two rabbits, and so on until December. Meanwhile, down the road at the Right On Rabbits! farm, the number of rabbits also doubles every month. However, the owner there did not begin raising rabbits until March. She began in March with one rabbit, and in April had two rabbits, and so on. At the end of December of the same year, how many rabbits are there at both Bunny Express and Right On Rabbits!? Justify your answer.

1. The graph of $y = x^2$ is given below.

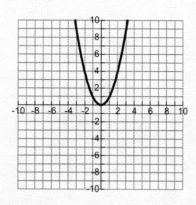

What is the vertex of the function $y = x^2 - 2$?

A. (0, 0)

B. (0, -2)

C. (0, 2)

D. (-2, 0)

2. The area of a triangle is $12x^6y^9$ square units. The base of the triangle is $6x^2y^3$ units. What is the height of the triangle in units?

A. $2x^4y^6$

B. $2x^3y^3$

C. $4x^4y^6$

D. $4x^3y^3$

3. The graph of $y = x^2$ is given below.

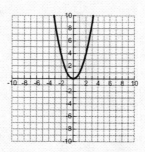

What function is graphed below?

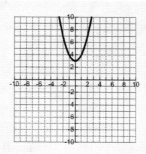

A. $y = (x + 3)^2$

B. $y = (x - 3)^2$

C. $y = x^2 + 3$

D. $y = x^2 - 3$

4. Which expression best represents the simplification of $(2x^2y^{-2}z)(-3x^{-1}y^{-2}z^3)$?

A. $\dfrac{-6xz^4}{y^4}$

B. $\dfrac{2xz^4}{3y^4}$

C. $\dfrac{2x^3}{3z^2}$

D. $\dfrac{-6x^3}{z^2}$

TAKS Mathematics Preparation Book: Grade 9

What's My Transformation I?

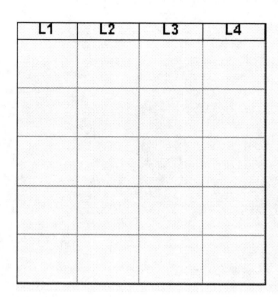

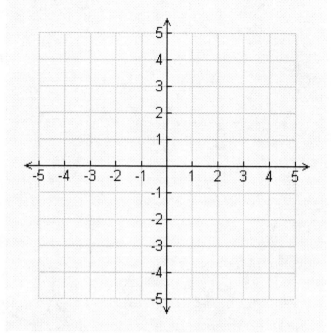

1. How is the second figure like the first figure?

2. What is different about the figures?

3. What do you think caused the figures to be in different locations?

4. How were the coordinates changed from the first to the second figure?

5. Create a new table of values that will maintain the shape and size of the original figure and move it to a different location.

6. Graph the new shape using your graphing calculator.

Activity Sheet 1

1. Record the vertices of quadrilateral ABCD in Table 1.

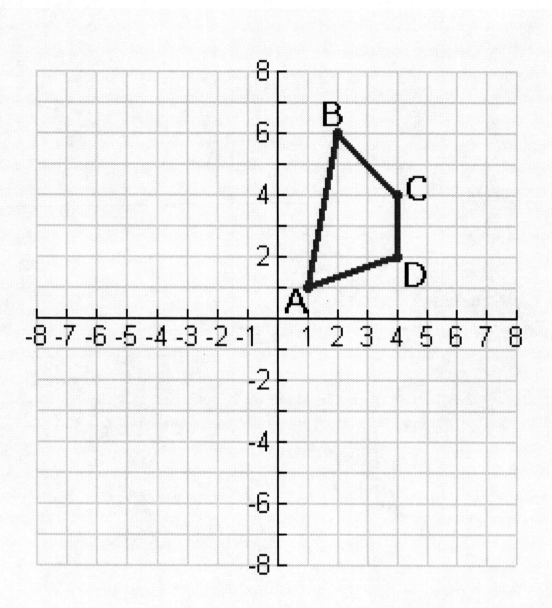

2. Place a sheet of patty paper (tracing paper) over the grid above.

3. Trace the quadrilateral and the axes. Label the quadrilateral A'B'C'D' .

4. Translate the quadrilateral five units to the left by sliding the patty (tracing) paper. Record the vertices of quadrilateral A'B'C'D' in Table 1.

Table 1	
Original Figure	**Original Image Translated Horizontally 5 units Left**
A (,)	A' (,)
B (,)	B' (,)
C (,)	C' (,)
(x, y)	(,)

5. What happened to the x-coordinates under the horizontal translation?

6. What happened to the y-coordinates under the horizontal translation?

7. What rule describes your horizontal translation?

8. Find the slopes of the sides of the original quadrilateral and the slopes of the sides of the translated image. Record the slopes in the table.

	Original Image	**Original Image Translated 5 Units Left**
slope AB		
slope BC		
slope CD		
slope DA		
Any	m	

9. Make a general statement that describes the effect on slope when an image is translated left.

10. Return the quadrilateral to its original position.

11. Record the vertices of quadrilateral ABCD in Table 2.

12. Translate the quadrilateral three units down by sliding the patty (tracing) paper. Record the vertices of quadrilateral A'B'C'D' in Table 2.

Table 2	
Original Figure	**Original Image Translated Vertically 3 units down**
A (,)	A' (,)
B (,)	B' (,)
C (,)	C' (,)
(x, y)	(,)

13. What happened to the x-coordinates under the vertical translation?

14. What happened to the y-coordinates under the vertical translation?

15. What rule describes your vertical translation?

16. Find the slopes of the sides of the original quadrilateral and the slopes of the sides of the translated image. Record the slopes in the table.

	Original Image	**Original Image Translated vertically 3 units down**
slope AB		
slope BC		
slope CD		
slope DA		
Any	m	

17. Make a general statement that describes the effect on slope when an image is translated vertically 3 units down.

18. Return the quadrilateral to its original position.

19. Record the vertices of quadrilateral ABCD in Table 3.

20. Translate the quadrilateral five units left then translate the new image three units down by sliding the patty (tracing) paper. Record the vertices of quadrilateral A'B'C'D' in Table 3.

	Table 3	
Original Figure	**Original Image Translated Horizontally 5 units Left**	**New Image Translated Vertically 3 units down**
A (,)	A' (,)	A" (,)
B (,)	B' (,)	B" (,)
C (,)	C' (,)	C" (,)
(x , y)	(x , y)	(,)

21. What happened to the *x*-coordinates under the composition of a horizontal and vertical translation?

22. What happened to the *y*-coordinates under the composition of a horizontal and vertical translation?

23. What rule describes your composition of a horizontal and vertical translation?

24. Find the slopes of the sides of the original quadrilateral and the slopes of the sides of the final translated image. Record the slopes in the table.

	Original Image	**Original Image Translated horizontally 5 units left and Vertically 3 units down**
slope AB		
slope BC		
slope CD		
slope DA		
Any	*m*	

25. Make a general statement that describes the effect on slope when an image is translated vertically 3 units down.

Activity 2

1. A triangle has vertices D (-2, 2), E (4, 4), and F (3, -4). If the triangle is translated by $(x + 2, y - 3)$, what will be the coordinates of the vertices of the new image?

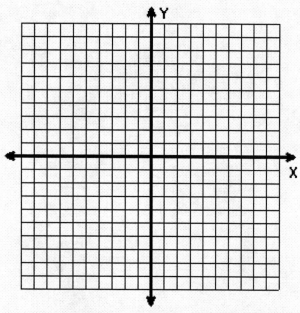

2. A quadrilateral with vertices F (-2, 5), O (5, 5), R (3, 1), and T (-4, 1) is translated so that a mapping of F to F′ locates F′ at (-5, 0). What are the coordinates of O′, R′, and T′?

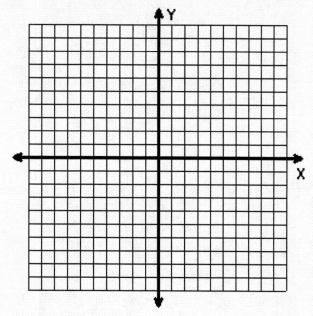

3. Jose performed the following translation for his math homework but can't find the original problem. What translation did he perform?

Original Figure	Translated Figure
A (-5, 12)	A' (1, 5)
B (7, -2)	B' (13, -9)
C (3, 8)	C' (10, 2)

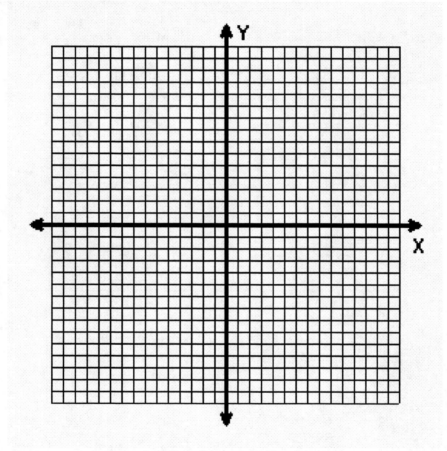

Write a verbal description of the translation.

Write an algebraic representation of the translation.

a. YES   NO   Student arrives at a correct solution?

	4	3	2	1
b. Conceptual Knowledge				
c. Procedural Knowledge				
d. Communication				

Mariela and her friend, Tracy, have a homework assignment. One problem has a quadrilateral with coordinates E (1, -1), F (5, -1), G (5, -3), H (1, -3) that is transformed under two translations. Mariela performed the translation $(x + 1, y + 5)$, and then the transformed the new image under the translation $(x - 6, y - 3)$. Tracy, on the other hand, transformed the original quadrilateral under the translation $(x - 6, y - 3)$ then transformed that image under the translation $(x + 1, y + 5)$. Whose translation is correct? Justify your answer.

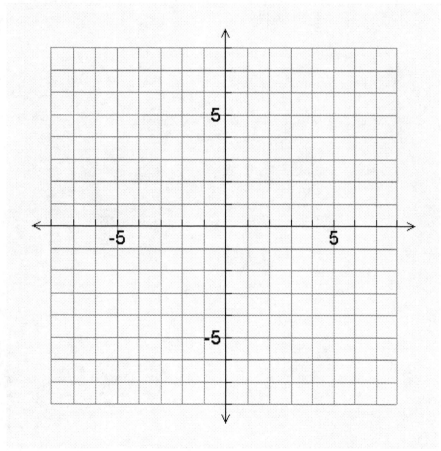

What's My Transformation II?

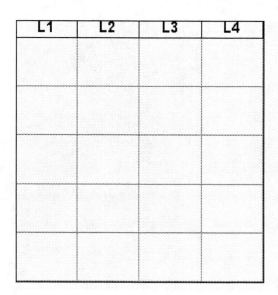

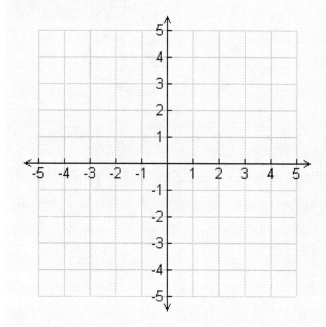

1. How is the second figure like the first figure?

2. What is different about the figures?

3. What do you think caused the figures to be in different locations?

4. How were the coordinates changed from the first to the second figure?

5. Create a new table of values that will maintain the shape and size of the original figure and move it to a different location?

6. Graph the new shape using your graphing calculator.

Activity 1: Triangle

All rotations are counterclockwise about the origin.

- Using a sheet of patty paper, trace your *x*- and *y*-axes and draw a triangle in Quadrant I of the coordinate plane. Record the coordinates of the vertices.

- Rotate the patty paper 90º and record the coordinates of each of the vertices of the rotated triangle.

- Now, rotate the patty paper 180º from the original position and record the coordinates of each of the vertices of the rotated triangle.

- Rotate the patty paper 270º from the original position and record the coordinates of each of the vertices of the rotated triangle.

- Finally, rotate the patty paper 360º from the original position and record the coordinates of each of the vertices of the rotated triangle.

Triangle Vertices	0º Rotation	90º Rotation	180º Rotation	270º Rotation	360º Rotation
A					
B					
C					
P(*x*, *y*)					

- Find the slopes of the sides of the original triangle and the slopes of the sides of each of the rotated images. Record the slopes in the table.

	0º Rotation	90º Rotation	180º Rotation	270º Rotation	360º Rotation
slope AB					
slope BC					
slope CA					
any	*m*				

Activity 2: Quadrilateral

All rotations are counterclockwise about the origin.

Using a new sheet of patty paper, trace your *x*- and *y*-axes and draw a quadrilateral. Repeat the same procedure as in Activity 1 to fill in the table.

Quadrilateral Vertices	0º Rotation	90º Rotation	180º Rotation	270º Rotation	360º Rotation
A					
B					
C					
D					
P(*x, y*)					

- Find the slopes of the sides of the original quadrilateral and the slopes of the sides of each of the rotated images. Record the slopes in the table.

	0º Rotation	90º Rotation	180º Rotation	270º Rotation	360º Rotation
slope AB					
slope BC					
slope CD					
slope DA					
any	*m*				

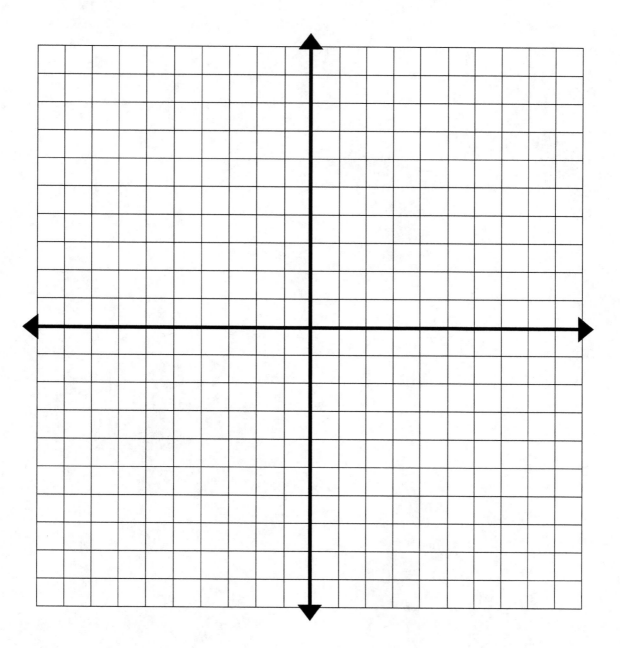

Questions for Discussion:

What patterns do you see in the ordered pairs?

Make a generalization about each of the four rotations:

➢ If a point P (x, y) is rotated 90º counterclockwise about the origin, the new ordered pair will be:

➢ If a point P (x, y) is rotated 180º counterclockwise about the origin, the new ordered pair will be:

➢ If a point P (x, y) is rotated 270º counterclockwise about the origin, the new ordered pair will be:

➢ If a point P (x, y) is rotated 360º counterclockwise about the origin, the new ordered pair will be:

Slope

➢ If a line segment is rotated 90º counterclockwise about the origin, how will the slope of the new segment compare to the slope of the original segment?

➢ If a line segment is rotated 180º counterclockwise about the origin, how will the slope of the new segment compare to the slope of the original segment?

➢ If a line segment is rotated 270º counterclockwise about the origin, how will the slope of the new segment compare to the slope of the original segment?

➢ If a line segment is rotated 360º counterclockwise about the origin, how will the slope of the new segment compare to the slope of the original segment?

Create a logo that is the result of rotating a quadrilateral 90º, 180º, and 270º about the origin.

Use coordinates to verify that each rotation is correct. Explain your process.

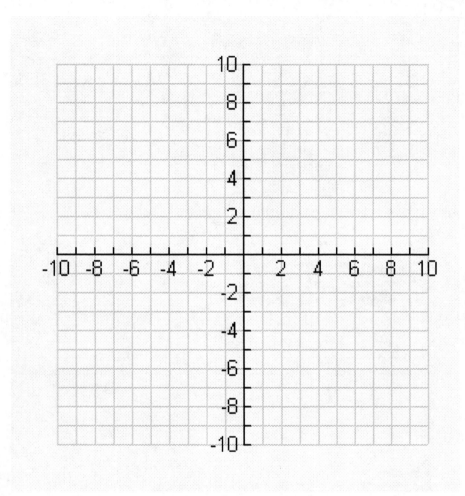

	4	3	2	1
b. Conceptual Knowledge				
c. Procedural Knowledge				
d. Communication				

Albert is designing a logo for his company. He wants to include two triangles, one of which is a rotation of the other. He performed a rotation of 270 degrees to obtain a rotated triangle with coordinates of (3, 1), (4, 4), and (1, 4). Unfortunately, he spilled coffee on the original triangle and only knows two of the original coordinates, (-4, 1) and (-4, 4). What is the third coordinate? Justify your answer.

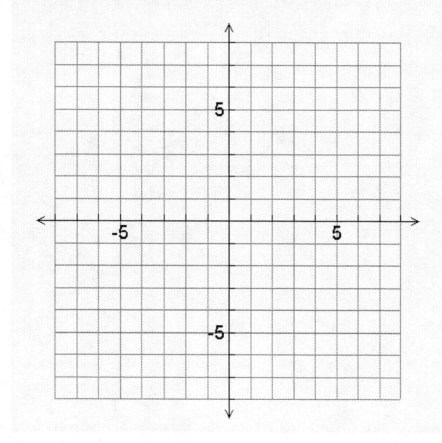

What's My Transformation III?

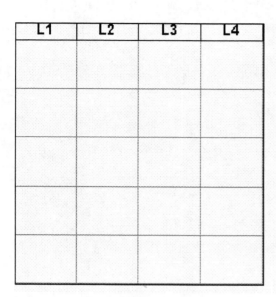

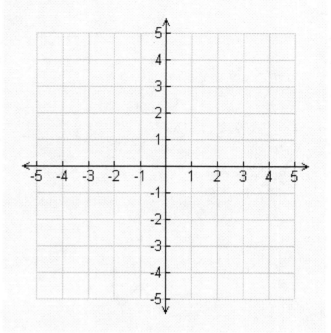

1. How is the second figure like the first figure?

2. What is different about the figures?

3. What do you think caused the figures to be in different locations?

4. How were the coordinates changed from the first to the second figure?

5. Create a new table of values that will maintain the shape and size of the original figure and move it to a different location?

6. Graph the new shape using your graphing calculator.

Activity 1: Reflections

1. Record the vertices of triangle ABC in Table 1.

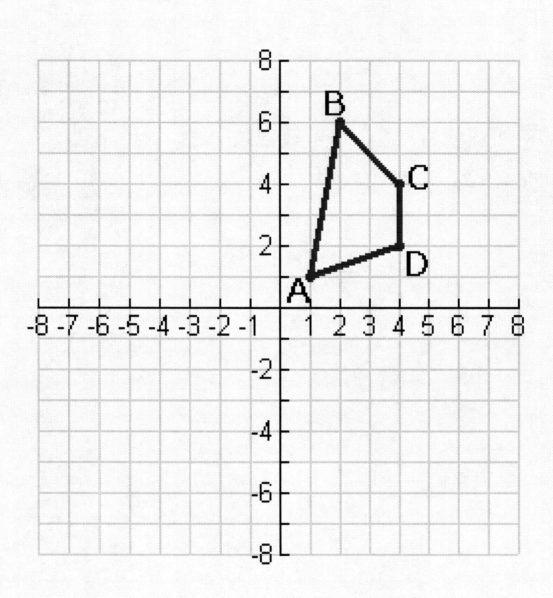

2. Place patty paper over grid paper.

3. Trace the quadrilateral and the axis. Label the quadrilateral A'B'C'D'.

4. Reflect the quadrilateral across the *y*-axis by flipping the patty paper. Record the vertices of quadrilateral A'B'C'D' in Table 1.

Table 1	
Original Figure	**Original Image Reflected Across the *y*-axis**
A (,)	A' (,)
B (,)	B' (,)
C (,)	C' (,)
D (,)	D' (,)
(*x*, *y*)	(,)

5. What happened to the *x*-coordinates under the reflection across the *y*-axis?

6. What happened to the *y*-coordinates under the reflection across the *y*-axis?

7. What rule describes the reflection across the *y*-axis?

8. Return the quadrilateral to its original position.

9. Record the vertices of quadrilateral ABCD in Table 2.

10. Reflect the quadrilateral across the *x*-axis by flipping the patty paper. Record the vertices of quadrilateral A'B'C'D' in Table 2.

Table 2	
Original Figure	**Original Image Reflected Across the x-axis**
A (,)	A' (,)
B (,)	B' (,)
C (,)	C' (,)
D (,)	D' (,)
(x, y)	(,)

11. What happened to the *x*-coordinates under the reflection across the *x*-axis?

12. What happened to the *y*-coordinates under the reflection across the *x*-axis?

13. What rule describes the reflection across the *x*-axis?

14. Find the slopes of the sides of the original quadrilateral and the slopes of the sides of the reflected images. Record the slopes in the table.

	Original Image	**Original Image Reflected Across the x-axis**	**Original Image Reflected Across the y-axis**
slope AB			
slope BC			
slope CD			
slope DA			
Any	*m*		

15. Make a general statement that describes the effect on slope when an image is reflected across the *x*-axis.

16. Make a general statement that describes the effect on slope when an image is reflected across the *y*-axis.

Activity 2

1. If a triangle with vertices D (-2, 2), E (4, 4), and F (3, -4) is reflected over the *y*-axis, what are the coordinates of the vertices of the new triangle image?

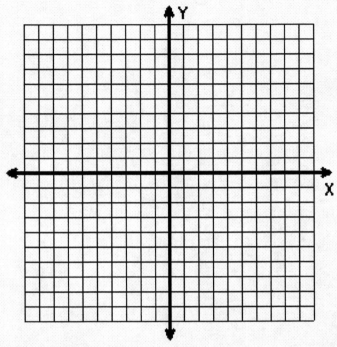

2. If a quadrilateral with vertices F (-2, 5), O (5, 5), R (3, 1), and T (-4, 1) is reflected over the *x*-axis, what are the coordinates of the vertices of the new image?

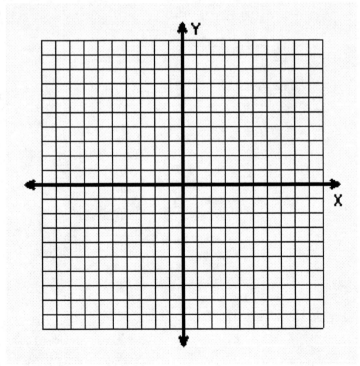

3. Maria performed the following reflection for her math homework but can't find the original problem. What reflection did she perform?

Original Figure	Reflected Figure
A (1, 1)	A' (-1, -1)
B (2, 4)	B' (-2, -4)
C (4, 2)	C' (-4, -2)

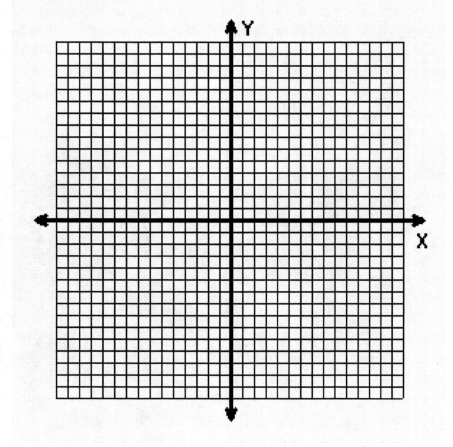

	4	3	2	1
b. Conceptual Knowledge				
c. Procedural Knowledge				
d. Communication				

A quadrilateral has coordinates E (1, -1), F (5, -1), G (5, -3), H (1, -3). Describe the reflection applied to the original quadrilateral if the intersection of the diagonals of the resulting quadrilateral is located at the point (-3, -2). Justify your answer.

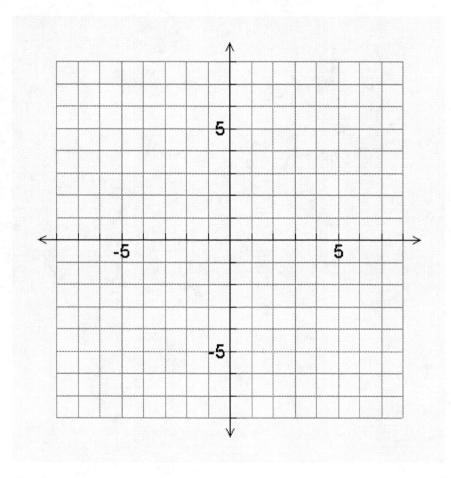

Activity 1

1. Record the vertices of △*DEF* in Table 1.

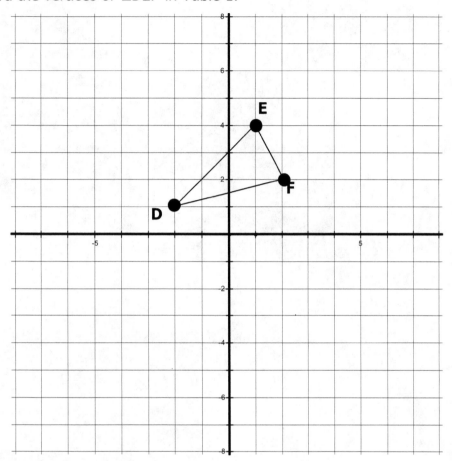

2. Draw Ray OD from the origin that extends beyond point D. Repeat for points E and F.

3. Use a piece of patty paper to mark the distance from the origin to point D. Measure this distance again along the ray beyond point D, and mark that new point, D', on the graph.

4. Use a piece of patty paper to mark the distance from the origin to point E. Measure this distance again along the ray beyond point E, and mark that new point, E', on the graph.

5. Use a piece of patty paper to mark the distance from the origin to point F. Measure this distance again along the ray beyond point F, and mark that new point, F', on the graph.

TAKS Mathematics Preparation Book: Grade 9

6. Connect points D′, E′, and F′ to create $\triangle D'E'F'$. Record the coordinates of D′, E′, and F′ in Table 1.

Table 1			
$\triangle DEF$		$\triangle D'E'F'$	
D		D′	
E		E′	
F		F′	

7. What patterns do you notice between the coordinates of $\triangle DEF$ and $\triangle D'E'F'$?

8. Measure the lengths of the sides in centimeters of $\triangle DEF$ and $\triangle D'E'F'$. Record this data in Table 2.

Table 2			
$\triangle DEF$		$\triangle D'E'F'$	
DE		D′E′	
EF		E′F′	
DF		D′F′	

9. What patterns do you notice between the side lengths of $\triangle DEF$ and $\triangle D'E'F'$?

10. Based on your data, what is the scale factor for this dilation?

11. Find the slopes of the sides of each of the triangles. Record the slopes in Table 3.

Table 3			
△**DEF**		△**D'E'F'**	
slope DE		slope D'E'	
slope EF		slope E'F'	
slope DF		slope D'F'	

12. How can you use the slopes in Table 3 to verify that there is a vanishing point for this situation?

Activity 2

1. On a clean sheet of graph paper, plot quadrilateral ASDF with vertices A (-1, 1), S (0, 5), D (4, 5), and F (3, 1).

2. Dilate this quadrilateral with a scale factor of 2. Label the dilated quadrilateral A'S'D'F'.

3. Record the coordinates of both quadrilaterals in the table.

Original Quadrilateral		Dilated Quadrilateral	
A	(,)	A'	(,)
S	(,)	S'	(,)
D	(,)	D'	(,)
F	(,)	F'	(,)

4. What patterns do you notice between the coordinates of the original quadrilateral and the dilated quadrilateral?

5. Either on another sheet of graph paper or with another color, plot a small triangle near the origin. Keep side lengths to 4 units or smaller. Label the vertices A, B, and C.

6. Dilate this triangle with a scale factor of 3. Label the corresponding vertices A', B', and C'.

7. Record the coordinates of both triangles in the table. What patterns do you notice?

Original Triangle			Dilated Triangle		
A	(	,)	A'	(	,)
B	(	,)	B'	(	,)
C	(	,)	C'	(	,)

8. Based on your data and what you have observed, make a conjecture for a rule that describes dilations from the origin in general.

a.   YES   NO   Student arrives at a correct solution?

	4	3	2	1
b. Conceptual Knowledge				
c. Procedural Knowledge				
d. Communication				

A video game designer is creating a new computer game. Before writing the program, she maps out one of the figures on grid paper. The vertices of the figure are (2, 3), (2, -5), and (-3, -5). During the game, the figure will move left 5 units and up 4 units. This figure also enlarges by a scale factor of 3 with the origin as the point of dilation to make another new figure. What are the coordinates of the new image? Justify your answer.

1. What is the scale factor that maps quadrilateral ABCD onto quadrilateral WXYZ with the center of dilation at (0, 0)?

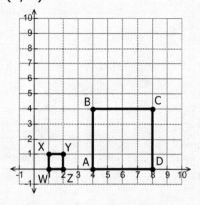

   A. $\dfrac{1}{4}$

   B. $\dfrac{1}{3}$

   C. 3

   D. 4

2. If triangle WXY is reflected across the *x*-axis, what shape would be formed by combining the original triangle and the new triangle?

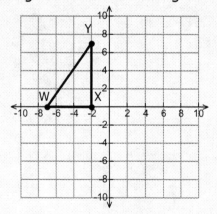

   A. An isosceles triangle

   B. A right triangle

   C. A rectangle

   D. An equilateral triangle

3. Triangle ABC is translated 2 units left and 4 units down. What are the coordinates for C'?

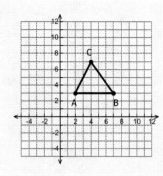

A. (2, 3)

B. (3, 2)

C. (5, 0)

D. (4, 7)

4. Which of the following statements is true about the points below?

$$(2, 2), (1, 2), (0, 2), (-1, 2), (-2, 2)$$

A. The points lie on the line $y = x$.

B. The points lie on the line $y = -x$.

C. The points lie on the line $y = 2$.

D. The points lie on the line $x = 2$.

How Do You See It? – ACTIVITY PART 1A

Build the following figure using blocks. Sketch the top, front, and right side views for each figure. Draw a three-dimensional image of the figure on the isometric grid. Could there be more than one solution? Justify your answer.

Figure #1:

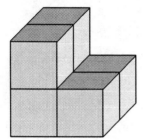

TOP View	FRONT View	RIGHT View

What is the surface area and volume of the building if each cube has a side length of 2 cm? Justify your answer.

What is the perimeter of the base? Justify your answer.

Build the following figure using blocks. Sketch the top, front, and right side views for each figure. Draw a three-dimensional image of the figure on the isometric grid. Could there be more than one solution? Justify your answer.

Figure #2:

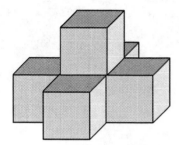

TOP View					FRONT View					RIGHT View				

What is the surface area and volume of the building if each cube has a side length of 2 cm? Justify your answer.

What is the perimeter of the base? Justify your answer.

Build the following figure using blocks. Sketch the top, front, and right side views for each figure. Draw a three-dimensional image of the figure on the isometric grid. Could there be more than one solution? Justify your answer.

Figure #3:

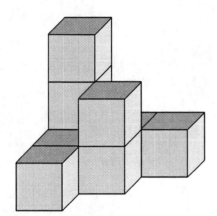

TOP View				FRONT View			RIGHT View		

What is the surface area and volume of the building if each cube has a side length of 2 cm? Justify your answer.

What is the perimeter of the base? Justify your answer.

How Do You See It? – ACTIVITY PART 1B

Build each of the following objects based on the views given. Draw a three-dimensional image of the figure on the isometric grid.

Figure #1:

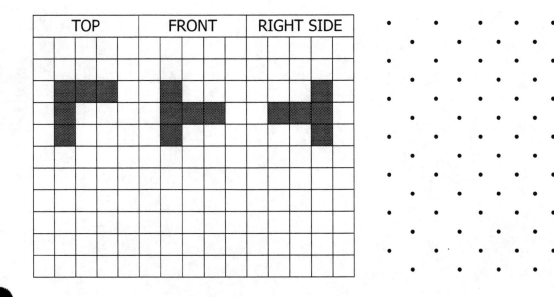

Figure #2:

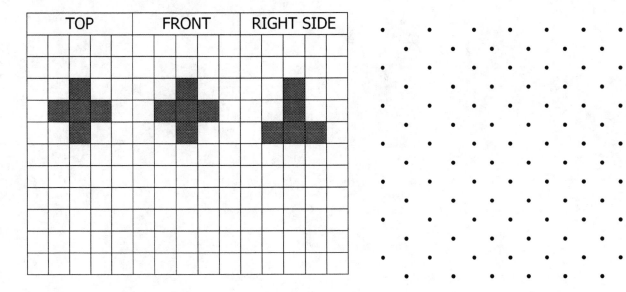

Term 1

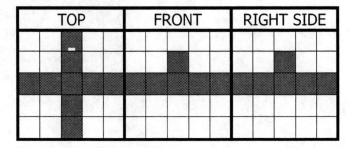

TOP	FRONT	RIGHT SIDE

Term 2

TOP	FRONT	RIGHT SIDE

Term 3

TOP	FRONT	RIGHT SIDE

1. Build the first five terms of the sequence using 2-cm cubes and determine the surface area for each term. The top, front, and side views for the first three terms are given.

2. Complete the table on the next page.

3. Graph the surface area vs. the term number.

4. Write a rule for the surface area of any term.

5. Find the surface area of the tenth term.

6. Which term has a surface area that is 1512 cm^2?

Student Name:_____   **Date:** _____

Term	Picture	Process	Surface Area (cm^2)
1			
2			
3			
4			
5			
10			
n			

TAKS Mathematics Preparation Book: Grade 9

BUILDING MAT

BACK

LEFT

RIGHT

FRONT

a.   YES   NO   Student arrives at a correct solution?

	4	3	2	1
b. Conceptual Knowledge				
c. Procedural Knowledge				
d. Communication				

Joey is building a stand for his electric keyboard. He wants the keyboard to sit 3 feet off the ground. The keyboard is 4.5 feet wide, and the stand is made using metal crossbars that are equal in length.

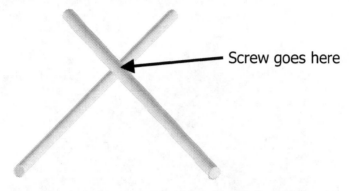

Screw goes here

If the screw to join the two metal poles is to be placed three-fourths of the way up each pole, how many inches from the bottom of each pole is the screw? Justify your answer.

1. The picture below is a two-dimensional solid built with cubes.

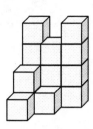

Which of the drawings below is the top view?

A.

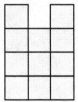

B.

C.

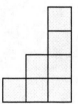

D.

TAKS Mathematics Preparation Book: Grade 9

310

2. A cellular phone tower can transmit a signal 49 miles in every direction. What is the total area the tower can service?

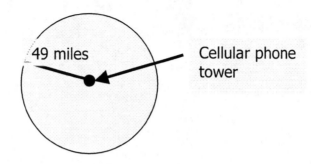

49 miles

Cellular phone tower

A. 98 square miles

B. 308 square miles

C. 2401 square miles

D. 7539 square miles

3. A bicycle tire has a diameter of 14 inches. How far does the tire travel in 10 revolutions?

A. 44 inches

B. 154 inches

C. 440 inches

D. 1540 inches

4. Margaret is constructing a model of the Pythagorean Theorem. She builds a model like the one shown below.

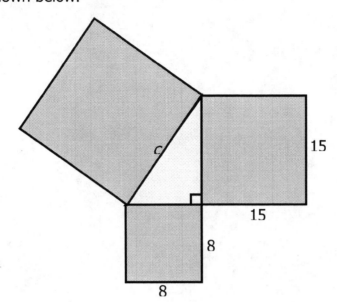

Which figure below represents the dimensions of c^2?

A.

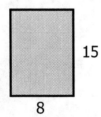

C.

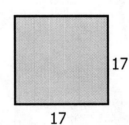

B.

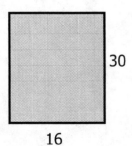

D.

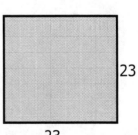

What's My Surface Area and Volume

.

Complete the following for each of your solids

1. **Cube**
   Surface Area:_____
   Shape of the base: _____
   Formula for Area of Base: _____
   Area of Base (*B*): _____
   Height of Solid (*h*): _____
   Formula for Volume: _____
   Volume of Solid: _____

Sketch the net and the solid.

2. **Rectangular Prism**
   Surface Area:_____
   Shape of the base: _____
   Formula for Area of Base: _____
   Area of Base *(B)*: _____
   Height of Solid *(h)*: _____
   Formula for Volume: _____
   Volume of Solid: _____

Sketch the net and the solid.

3. **Cylinder**
   Surface Area:_____
   Shape of the base: _____
   Formula for Area of Base: _____
   Area of Base *(B)*: _____
   Height of Solid *(h)*: _____
   Formula for Volume: _____
   Volume of Solid: _____

Sketch the net and the solid.

4. **Cone**
   Surface Area:_____
   Shape of the base: _____
   Formula for Area of Base: _____
   Area of Base *(B)*: _____
   Height of Solid *(h)*: _____
   Formula for Volume: _____
   Volume of Solid: _____

Sketch the net and the solid.

Determine and apply the appropriate formula for these solids.

5. **Name of solid:** _____
   Surface Area:_____
   Shape of the base: _____
   Formula for Area of Base: _____
   Area of Base *(B)*: _____
   Height of Solid *(h)*: _____
   Formula for Volume: _____
   Volume of Solid: _____

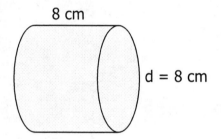

8 cm

d = 8 cm

Sketch the net.

6. **Square Pyramid**
   Surface Area:_____
   Shape of the base: _____
   Formula for Area of Base: _____
   Area of Base *(B)*: _____
   Height of Solid *(h)*: _____
   Formula for Volume: _____
   Volume of Solid: _____

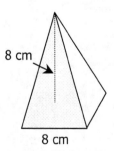

8 cm

8 cm

Sketch the net.

7. **Name of solid:** _____
   Surface Area:_____
   Shape of the base: _____
   Formula for Area of Base: _____
   Area of Base *(B)*: _____
   Height of Solid *(h)*: _____
   Formula for Volume: _____
   Volume of Solid: _____

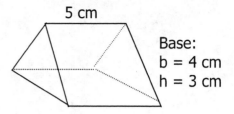

Base:
b = 4 cm
h = 3 cm

Sketch the net.

8. **Name of solid:** _____

   Surface Area:_____

   Formula for Volume: _____

   Volume of Solid: _____

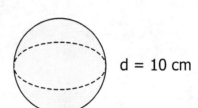

d = 10 cm

Volume Applications

1. Use a centimeter ruler to measure the dimensions of the net below. Use your measurements to find the surface area and volume of the solid that the net will form.

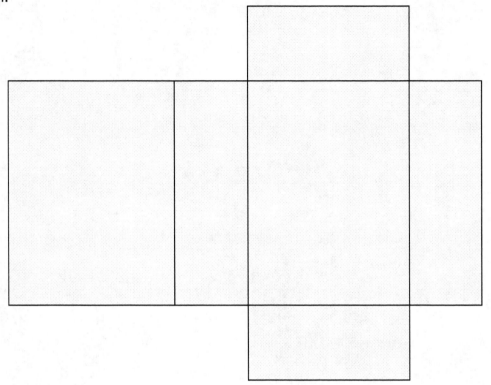

2. If all of the dimensions of the net were doubled, what would be the surface area and volume of the solid?

3. A milk storage tank on the Sweet Milk Farm is in the shape of a cylinder. The height of the tank is 15 feet and the diameter is 8 feet. If there are 7.48 gallons in a cubic foot, how many gallons does the storage tank hold? Justify your answer.

4. A conical paper drinking cup is 12 centimeters in height and holds approximately 113 cubic centimeters of liquid. What is the approximate radius of the cup? Justify your answer.

5. A shipping box for a racquetball manufacturer measures 2 feet by 1 foot with a height of 1 foot. The racquetballs are packaged in cylindrical containers that have a diameter of 3 inches and a height of 11 inches. What is the greatest number of racquetball containers that will fix in the shipping box? Justify your answer.

6. Which container will hold more: a can that has a diameter of 4 inches and a height of 4.5 inches or a can that has a diameter of 3 inches and a height of 8 inches? Justify your answer.

7. A company sells two types of boxes of cereal that are shaped like rectangular prisms. The larger cereal box has a volume of 1658 cubic centimeters. The smaller cereal box has dimensions that are half the size of the larger box. What is the volume, in cubic centimeters, of the smaller box? Justify your answer.

8. A scale model of a new toy fits in a cube-shaped box shown below.

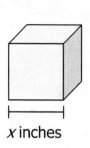

x inches

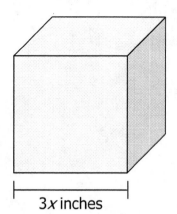

3x inches

The volume of the smaller box is 27 cubic inches. When the toy is manufactured, it will be packaged in a cube-shaped box whose dimensions are three times the dimensions of the smaller box. What is the volume, in cubic inches, of the larger box? Justify your answer.

a.   YES   NO   Student arrives at a correct solution?

	4	3	2	1
b. Conceptual Knowledge				
c. Procedural Knowledge				
d. Communication				

Mrs. Sandly asked her students to create a cylinder to hold chocolate candies for a statistics problem using a standard piece of paper (8.5 inches by 11 inches). Some of the students made cylinders that were 11 inches tall, and others created cylinders that were 8.5 inches tall. The students in Mrs. Sandly's class began having a discussion regarding the amount of chocolate candies that each person could store. Oliver said that each cylinder would hold the same amount of chocolate candies because all of them used the same size paper, but others disagreed. Who is correct? Justify your answer.

1. A rice company uses cardboard boxes to put the rice in to sell to customers. The net of the box looks like the figure below.

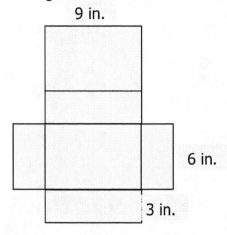

9 in.

6 in.

3 in.

How much cardboard does it take to make a box for the rice?

A. 252 square inches

B. 198 square inches

C. 162 square inches

D. 99 square inches

2. Nancy bought a present for her brother. The dimensions of the box were $24\frac{3}{4}$ inches by $10\frac{1}{2}$ inches by 14 inches. If Nancy bought wrapping paper to cover the box, approximately how much wrapping paper did she buy?

A. 3850 square inches

B. 1558 square inches

C. 1008 square inches

D. 779 square inches

3. Paul leans a 17-foot ladder against his house. If he places the base of the ladder 8 feet from the house, at what height will the top of the ladder rest against the house?

    A. 25 feet

    B. 19 feet

    C. 15 feet

    D. 9 feet

4. The scale on a map is 2 centimeters equals 20 miles. If the distance on the map between two cities is 18 centimeters, what is the actual distance between the two cities?

    A. 1.8 miles

    B. 40 miles

    C. 180 miles

    D. 360 miles

5. Veronica's bedroom has an area of 96 ft². She made a scale drawing of her bedroom to use to plan how to arrange the furniture in her room. If Veronica reduced the dimensions by $\frac{1}{8}$, what is the area of the scale drawing of her room?

    A. 12 square feet

    B. 8 square feet

    C. 6 square feet

    D. 1.5 square feet

6. A small cylinder has a volume of 188 mm^3. A larger cylinder has dimensions that are three times the dimensions of the smaller cylinder. What is the volume of the large cylinder?

A. 324 mm^3

B. 648 mm^3

C. 972 mm^3

D. 2916 mm^3

The Great Race Activity 1

Use the color tiles to represent the racecars. The rules are: car one moves when a one, two, three or four is rolled; and car two moves when a five, or six is rolled. The course is two sections long. The winner is the car that reaches the finish line first.

Race	Winner		Race	Winner		Race	Winner
1			39			77	
2			40			78	
3			41			79	
4			42			80	
5			43			81	
6			44			82	
7			45			83	
8			46			84	
9			47			85	
10			48			86	
11			49			87	
12			50			88	
13			51			89	
14			52			90	
15			53			91	
16			54			92	
17			55			93	
18			56			94	
19			57			95	
20			58			96	
21			59			97	
22			60			98	
23			61			99	
24			62			100	
26			63				
27			64				
28			66				
29			67				
30			68				
31			69				
32			70				
33			71				
34			72				
35			73				
36			74				
37			75				
38			76				

Experimental probability of car 1 winning:

_____

The Great Race Activity 1

Track

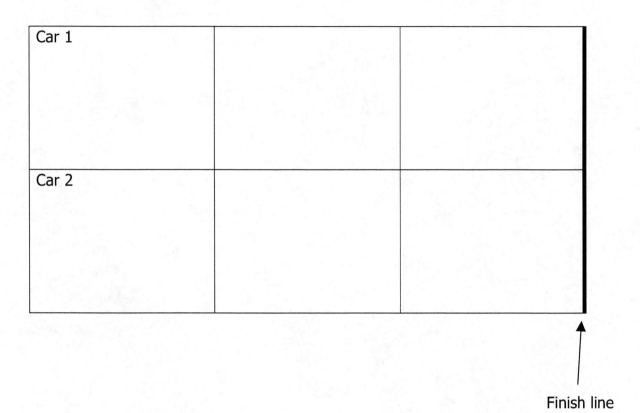

Finish line

The Great Race Activity 2

Use the color tiles to represent the racecars. The rules are: car one moves when a one, two, three or four is rolled; and car two moves when a five, or six is rolled. The course is three sections long. The winner is the car that reaches the finish line first.

Race	Winner		Race	Winner		Race	Winner
1			39			77	
2			40			78	
3			41			79	
4			42			80	
5			43			81	
6			44			82	
7			45			83	
8			46			84	
9			47			85	
10			48			86	
11			49			87	
12			50			88	
13			51			89	
14			52			90	
15			53			91	
16			54			92	
17			55			93	
18			56			94	
19			57			95	
20			58			96	
21			59			97	
22			60			98	
23			61			99	
24			62			100	
26			63				
27			64				
28			66				
29			67				
30			68				
31			69				
32			70				
33			71				
34			72				
35			73				
36			74				
37			75				
38			76				

Experimental probability of car 1 winning:

_____

The Great Race Activity 2

Track

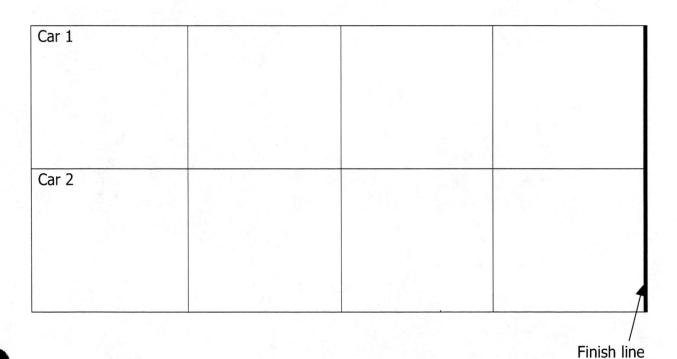

1. Determine the experimental probability of car 1 winning for 100 trials.

2. Determine the possible race scenarios.

3. Determine the theoretical probability of car 1 winning.

4. Based on your findings what would you predict the probability of car one winning if the track had four sections? Five? Why?

a.　　YES　　NO　　Student arrives at a correct solution?

	4	3	2	1
b. Conceptual Knowledge				
c. Procedural Knowledge				
d. Communication				

Four girls and four boys sit around a merry-go-round. If they seat themselves at random, what is the probability that boys and girls will alternate?

Gridiron

September - October Statistics for Steven Scooter

Date of Game	Total Yards
Sept. 4	56
Sept. 11	44
Sept. 18	92
Sept. 25	107
Oct. 2	75
Oct. 9	32
Oct. 16	102
Oct. 23	98
Oct. 30	94

Steven wants to be traded. The above table lists his total yards gained for his team during the months of September and October. Use the best measure of central tendency (mean, median, or mode) to write a brief description of Steven's abilities. Steven will use this description to help promote himself to other teams.

Ruth vs. McGwire

Look at a comparison of the number of home runs hit each season by baseball stars Babe Ruth and Mark McGwire.

Babe Ruth (1920 - 1934)

54	59	35	41	46	25	47	60	54	46	49
46	41	34	22							

Mark McGwire (1987 - 1999)

49	32	33	39	22	42	9	9	39	52	58
70	65									

1. Find the mean, median, and the mode for this set of data.

2. Which measure of central tendency would you use to compare their scores and why?

3. Create histograms for each player's data sets. Sketch them below.

4. How many home runs would Mark McGwire have to hit in each of the next five seasons in order for his median to be the same as Babe Ruth's?

5. How many home runs would Mark McGwire have to hit in each of the next five seasons in order for his mean to be the same as Babe Ruth's?

a.   YES   NO   Student arrives at a correct solution?

	4	3	2	1
b. Conceptual Knowledge				
c. Procedural Knowledge				
d. Communication				

The owner of "You Want It, We Got It" produced a report with the following information about his store's payroll.

# of employees	Job Title	Yearly Salary
10	Maintenance Crew	$14,500
11	Sales Representative	$17,000
8	Cashier	$19,500
4	Manager	$47,500
1	Owner	$80,000

The non-managerial employees have asked the owner for a raise. The owner feels that they are making a good salary and do not need a raise. You have been assigned as the arbitrator who will decide whether or not the non-managerial employees should receive a raise. The employees who are asking for a raise have noted that the average salary for non-managerial employees at competing companies is $20,000. Should the employees receive a raise? Justify your answer.

Youth Poll

A poll was conducted to determine the topics teenagers most want to discuss with their parents. The poll was based on a national sample of 505 teenagers selected at random. The results are shown in the graph below.

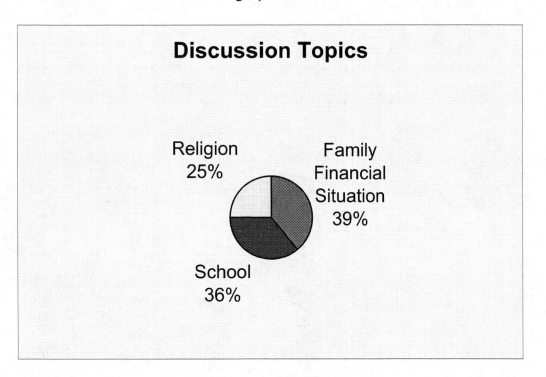

Discussion Topics

Religion 25%

Family Financial Situation 39%

School 36%

Create a different graph to display the same set of data. Justify your choice of graph.

In a recent survey of driving adults from across the United States 1756 people were randomly sampled to determine their preference in automobile manufacturer.
720 people chose General Motors, 615 people chose Ford, 421 people chose Chrysler.

Create a circle graph to represent this data.

1. What information did the problem give you?

2. How can you change the responses to percentages?

3. Find the number of degrees in each central angle.

4. Construct your graph.

a.   YES   NO   Student arrives at a correct solution?

	4	3	2	1
b. Conceptual Knowledge				
c. Procedural Knowledge				
d. Communication				

The video store where you work is getting ready to create a new advertising campaign in order to increase business. To be cost effective, the video store wants to target one particular age group. Your boss has asked you to summarize the data on the ages of customers for one day with some sort of a graph.

Customers were asked to provide their ages as they rented their videos. Their responses are recorded below.

16	48	27	36	20	39	31	30
26	52	19	31	62	75	64	35
39	34	56	26	37	36	36	34
25	18	42	42	31	30	28	26
34	18	43	17	27	29	42	51
33	35	35	36	25	55	34	37
31	32	40	21	37	28	49	17
20	35	19	19	44	51	48	30

Construct a circle graph, bar graph, or histogram to best represent a summary of the data. Justify your answer.

1. Laurence mailed a package to his son for Christmas. The package weighed 15 pounds and cost $37.50 to mail. The shipping company charges the same rate per pound to mail a package. If Laurence also has a 22-pound package to mail, which proportion would give him the cost, c, to mail this package?

   A. $\dfrac{15}{22} = \dfrac{c}{37.50}$

   B. $\dfrac{15}{37.50} = \dfrac{22}{c}$

   C. $\dfrac{15}{37.50} = \dfrac{c}{22}$

   D. $\dfrac{15}{c} = \dfrac{22}{37.50}$

2. Barbara bought a coat at the mall. The cost of the coat was $140 before sales tax. If the total cost of the coat including tax was $150.50, what was the rate of the sales tax?

   A. 10.5%

   B. 8.25%

   C. 7.5%

   D. 6.9%

3. A gumball machine contains 5 green gumballs, 3 red gumballs, and 2 yellow gumballs. If Charlie buys 2 gumballs, what is the probability that one will be red and the other will be green?

   A. $\dfrac{8}{10}$

   B. $\dfrac{3}{5}$

   C. $\dfrac{1}{6}$

   D. $\dfrac{3}{20}$

4. The results of a survey on favorite restaurants are given in the table below.

Restaurant A	Restaurant B	Restaurant C
卌 卌	卌 |||	卌 ||

Which of the following statements would best describe the results if the survey were expanded to include 100 participants?

A. 7 would choose Restaurant C.

B. Twice as many people would prefer Restaurant A to Restaurant C.

C. 40% of the people would choose Restaurant A.

D. The number of people choosing Restaurant B and Restaurant C would equal those choosing Restaurant A.

5. The circle graph shows the ages of people who bought a ticket for a particular movie over the weekend.

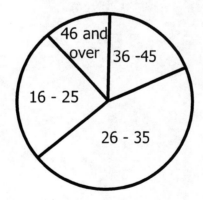

If 650 people bought tickets to the movie, how many of them were between the ages of 16 – 25?

A. 325

C. 160

B. 216

D. 41

a.   YES   NO   Student arrives at a correct solution?

	4	3	2	1
b. Conceptual Knowledge				
c. Procedural Knowledge				
d. Communication				

A brick company manufactures decorative bricks in the shape of isosceles trapezoids. The longer base of the smallest trapezoid is 20 cm. The legs of this trapezoid are 4 cm long each, and the trapezoid has a perimeter of 43 cm.

The next larger trapezoid has the same base lengths as the first, and has a perimeter of 51 cm.

The third trapezoid in the series has the same base lengths as the other two, and a perimeter of 67 cm.

If this pattern continues, find the area of the tenth brick. Justify your answer.

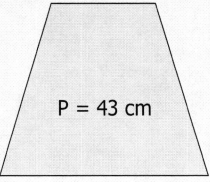

P = 43 cm

a.   YES   NO   Student arrives at a correct solution?

	4	3	2	1
b. Conceptual Knowledge				
c. Procedural Knowledge				
d. Communication				

An architectural firm has been hired by the City Council to design a rock garden for a new park in the business district. The rock garden is a pentagon whose sides are defined by the following five equations:

$$x = -3$$
$$y = -3$$
$$y = 2x - 5$$
$$x - 3y = -12$$
$$x + y = 4$$

One bag of rocks for the garden costs $17.95 and will cover 2 ft^2. On the coordinate plane, each unit represents one foot. The city has allocated $350 for materials for this project. Will the architect's design fit into the materials budget for the rock garden?

1. Virginia graphed the system of equations shown below.

$$y = x + 6$$

$$y = 2x + 5$$

She determined that the solution to the system was (1, 7).

If Virginia translated both lines up 2 units, what would be the solution to the new system of equations?

A. (1, 7)

B. (3, 7)

C. (1, 9)

D. (3, 9)

2. Maureen wants to cut a circle out of a square piece of paper as shown in the drawing below.

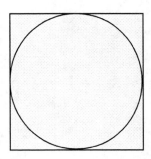

If she knows the length of the side of the square, how can she calculate the area of the circle?

A. Square the length of the side of the square and multiply the answer by π.

B. Divide the length of the side of the square by 2 to get the length of the length of the radius. Square the length of the radius and then multiply the answer by π.

C. Multiply the length of the side of the square by π.

D. Square the length of the side of the square.

3. Carolyn wants to earn at least $245 in order to buy a television for her bedroom. She already has $50 in a savings account. In addition, she is earning $6 an hour at her part-time job. Which of the following inequalities could she use to find h the number of hours she must work in order to earn the amount of money she wants?

   A. $50 + 6x \leq 245$

   B. $50 + 6x \geq 245$

   C. $50x + 6 \leq 245$

   D. $50x + 6 \geq 245$

4. Travis found a bicycle he wanted to buy that costs $134.50. He has a coupon he can use that will save him 20% off the original price. Travis has $89.60 in his savings account and earns $5.50 an hour at his job.

   Arrange the steps in the order that Travis can use to calculate how many more hours he must work in order to have enough money to buy the bicycle.

   W Subtract the amount of discount from the original price of the bicycle to find the sales price of the bicycle.

   X Divide the amount of money Travis still needs to buy the bicycle by 5.5 to determine the number of hours he must work.

   Y Multiply the original cost of the bicycle by 20% to find the amount of discount.

   Z Subtract the amount of money Travis has in his savings account from the sales price to determine how much more money he needs to buy the bicycle.

   A. Y, W, Z, X

   B. Z, Y, X, W

   C. X, Y, W, Z

   D. W, X, Y, Z

5. Mary drove 195 miles in 3 hours. The number of miles, *m*, which Mary can drive in *h* hours, can be found by _____

   A. multiplying *h* by 195

   B. multiplying 195 by 3 and multiplying by *h*

   C. dividing *h* by *m*

   D. dividing 195 by 3 and multiplying by *h*

6. The graphs of the lines $x = -3$, $y = 2$, and $y = 2x - 2$ intersect to form a triangle. What is the area of the triangle formed by the three intersecting lines?

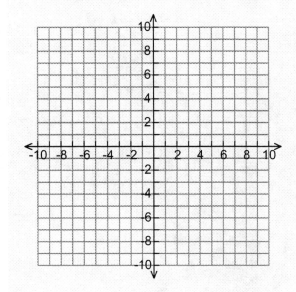

   A. 5

   B. 10

   C. 25

   D. 50

7. Charlie has a fish tank that is a rectangular prism. The dimensions of the tank are 24 inches long, 10 inches wide, and 14 inches tall. If Charlie only filled the tank half full of water, which equation below could he use to calculate the amount of water, W, in the tank?

A. $\frac{1}{2}(24 \bullet 10 \bullet 14) = W$

B. $\frac{1}{2}(24) \bullet \frac{1}{2}(10) \bullet \frac{1}{2}(14) = W$

C. $24 \bullet 10 \bullet 14 = W$

D. $\frac{1}{2}(24) \bullet \frac{1}{2}(10) \bullet \frac{1}{2}(14) = \frac{1}{2}W$

8. Megan wants to determine how much wrapping paper she will need to wrap a present that is a rectangular prism. Which formula would be best for Megan to use to calculate how much paper she needs to wrap the present?

A. Volume of a prism

B. Total Surface Area of a prism

C. Lateral Area of a prism

D. Area of a rectangle

9. The graphs of two equations are shown below.

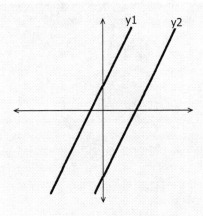

Which of the following statements is true about the graphs?

A. The y-intercepts of the two lines are the same.

B. The y-intercept of y2 is positive.

C. The slope of y1 is larger than the slope of y2.

D. The slopes of the two lines are the same.

Mathematics Performance Assessment Rubric

Part a) Correct Solution YES NO

Criteria	4	3	2	1
Part b) **Conceptual Knowledge**	**Attribute(s) of concept(s)** Correctly identifies attributes of the problem, which leads to correct inferences. **Inferences** Combines the critical attributes of the problem in order to describe correctly the mathematical relationship(s) inherent in the problem.	**Attribute(s) of concept(s)** Correctly identifies attributes of the problem, which leads to correct inferences. **Inferences** Combines the critical attributes of the problem, which leads to a partial identification of the mathematical relationship(s) inherent in the problem.	**Attribute(s) of concept(s)** Identifies some of the attributes of the problem, which leads to partially correct inferences. **Inferences** Combines the identified attributes of the problem, which leads to a partial identification of the mathematical relationship(s) inherent in the problem.	**Attribute(s) of concept(s)** Lacks identification of any of the critical attributes of the problem. **Inferences** Combines few of the attributes of the problem which leads to an incomplete identification of the mathematical relationship(s) inherent in the problem.
Part c) **Procedural Knowledge**	**Appropriate strategy** Selects and implements an appropriate strategy. **Representational form** Uses appropriate representation to connect the procedure to the concept of the problem. **Algorithmic competency** Correctly implements procedure to arrive at a correct solution.	**Appropriate strategy** Selects and implements an appropriate strategy. **Representational form** Uses appropriate representation to connect the procedure to the concept of the problem. **Algorithmic competency** Implements selected procedure but arrives at an incorrect solution.	**Appropriate strategy** Selects and implements an appropriate strategy. **Representational form** Uses inconsistent or insufficient representation for the selected solution strategy. **Algorithmic competency** Implements selected procedure but arrives at an incorrect or correct solution. (See Part a above)	**Appropriate strategy** Selects and implements an inappropriate strategy. **Representational form** Uses incorrect representations. **Algorithmic competency** Makes significant errors.
Part d) **Communication**	**Justification** Fully answers the question of "why" for the strategy selection; explains procedure; and/or evaluates reasonableness of solution. **Terminology** Uses appropriate terminology and notation.	**Justification** Fully answers the question of "why" for the strategy selection; explains procedure; and/or evaluates reasonableness of solution. **Terminology** Uses some appropriate terminology or notation.	**Justification** Incompletely answers the question of "why" for the strategy selection; explains procedure; and/or evaluates reasonableness of solution. **Terminology** Uses some appropriate terminology or notation.	**Justification** Provides very little or no explanation of what was done and why. **Terminology** Uses limited or inappropriate terminology or notation.

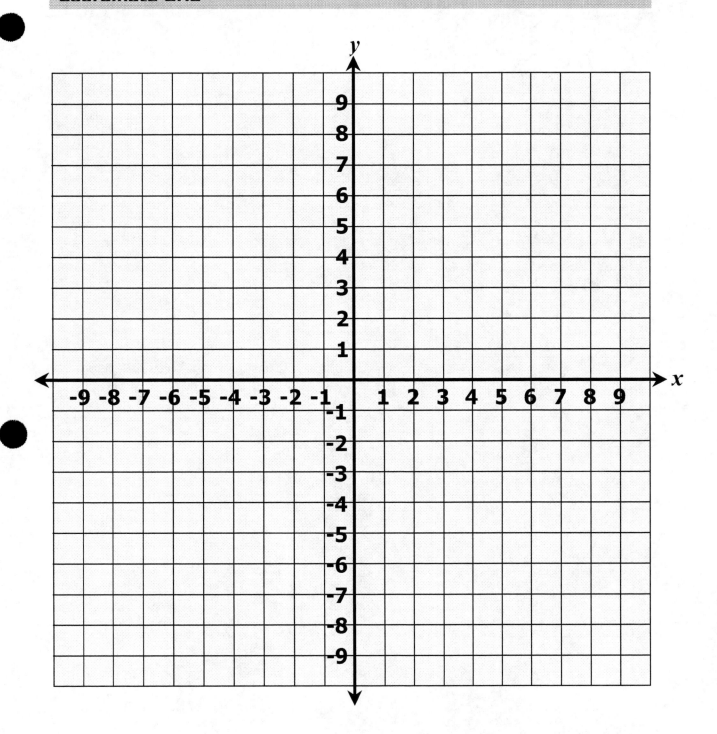

ISOMETRIC GRID PAPER

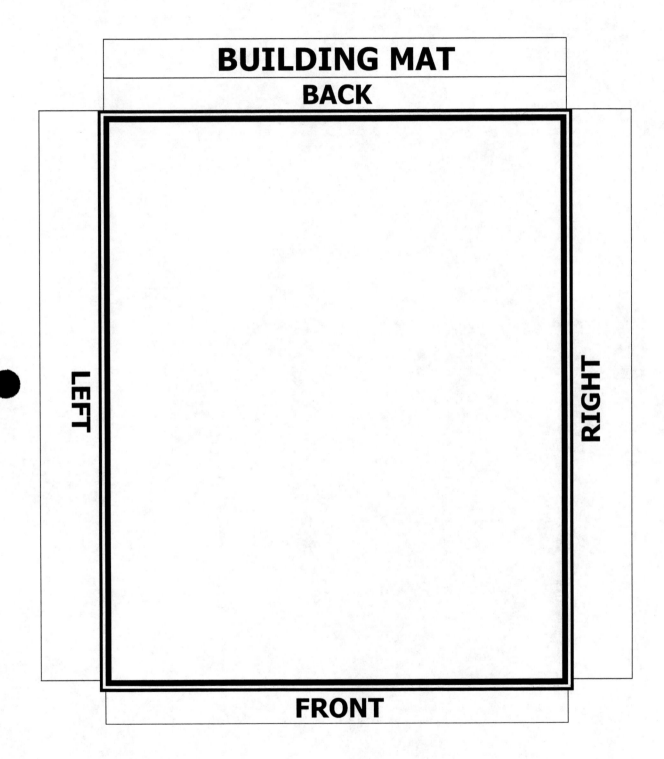

BUILDING MAT

BACK

LEFT

RIGHT

FRONT

TAKS Mathematics Preparation Series - English

**Education Service Center
Houston, Texas**

To Order by Mail:
Region IV ESC
Math/Science/Social Studies Services
7145 West Tidwell
Houston, TX 77092-2096

To Order by Fax:
713-744-6522
Math/Science/Social Studies Services

Please allow 2-4 weeks for delivery

Mailing Address

District _____

School _____

Attention: _____

Address _____

City _____ State _____ ZIP _____

Phone # _____

Billing Address
(if different from mailing address)

District _____

School _____

Attention: _____

Address _____

City _____ State _____ ZIP _____

Phone # _____

Method of Payment

☐ Purchase Order # _____
(attach to order)

☐ Visa   # _____

☐ MasterCard   # _____

Exp Date ____ / ____

☐ Check # _____   Amt $ _____

Amt $ _____

Signature Required _____

TEACHER EDITION WITH BLACKLINE MASTERS Prices good through August 2004	PRICE	QTY	AMOUNT
**TAKS Mathematics Preparation Grade K	$50.00		$
* *TAKS Mathematics Preparation Grade 1	$50.00		$
* *TAKS Mathematics Preparation Grade 2	$50.00		$
TAKS Mathematics Preparation Grade 3	$50.00		$
TAKS Mathematics Preparation Grade 4	$50.00		$
TAKS Mathematics Preparation Grade 5	$50.00		$
TAKS Mathematics Preparation Grade 6	$50.00		$
TAKS Mathematics Preparation Grade 7	$50.00		$
TAKS Mathematics Preparation Grade 8	$50.00		$
TAKS Mathematics Preparation Grade 9	$50.00		$
TAKS Mathematics Preparation Grade 10	$50.00		$
TAKS Mathematics Preparation Grade 11 Exit	$50.00		$
Subtotal			$

PRINTED STUDENT WORKBOOK Prices good through August 2004	PRICE	QTY	AMOUNT
** Class set of 30 Grade K	$360.00		$
** Class set of 30 Grade 1	$360.00		$
** Class set of 30 Grade 2	$360.00		$
*Class set of 30 Grade 3	$360.00		$
*Class set of 30 Grade 4	$360.00		$
*Class set of 30 Grade 5	$360.00		$
*Class set of 30 Grade 6	$360.00		$
*Class set of 30 Grade 7	$360.00		$
*Class set of 30 Grade 8	$360.00		$
*Class set of 30 Grade 9	$360.00		$
*Class set of 30 Grade 10	$360.00		$
*Class set of 30 Grade 11 Exit	$360.00		$
Subtotal			$
For shipping charges add 10% of total order; $5.00 minimum charge			$
TOTAL			$

* Teacher Edition must be ordered.

** Available June 2004

Bill McKinney, Ph.D., Executive Director
Region IV ESC is an equal opportunity employer

TAKS Mathematics Preparation Series - Spanish

REGION IV
Education Service Center
Houston, Texas

To Order by Mail:
Region IV ESC
Math/Science/Social Studies Services
7145 West Tidwell
Houston, TX 77092-2096

To Order by Fax:
713-744-6522
Math/Science/Social Studies Services

Please allow 2-4 weeks for delivery

Method of Payment

☐ Purchase Order # _____
(attach to order)

☐ Visa   # _____
☐ MasterCard   # _____

☐ Check # _____   Amt $ _____

Exp Date ____ / ____

Signature Required _____

Mailing Address

District _____
School _____
Attention: _____
Address _____

City _____ State _____ ZIP _____

Phone # _____

Amt $ _____

Billing Address
(if different from mailing address)

District _____
School _____
Attention: _____
Address _____

City _____ State _____ ZIP _____

Phone # _____

TEACHER EDITION WITH BLACKLINE MASTERS Prices good through August 2004	PRICE	QTY	AMOUNT
** Spanish TAKS Mathematics Preparation Grade K	$50.00		$
* * Spanish TAKS Mathematics Preparation Grade 1	$50.00		$
** Spanish TAKS Mathematics Preparation Grade 2	$50.00		$
Spanish TAKS Mathematics Preparation Grade 3	$50.00		$
Spanish TAKS Mathematics Preparation Grade 4	$50.00		$
Spanish TAKS Mathematics Preparation Grade 5	$50.00		$
Spanish TAKS Mathematics Preparation Grade 6	$50.00		$
		Subtotal	$

PRINTED STUDENT WORKBOOK Prices good through August 2004	PRICE	QTY	AMOUNT
** Spanish Class set of 30 Grade K	$360.00		$
** Spanish Class set of 30 Grade 1	$360.00		$
** Spanish Class set of 30 Grade 2	$360.00		$
* Spanish Class set of 30 Grade 3	$360.00		$
* Spanish Class set of 30 Grade 4	$360.00		$
* Spanish Class set of 30 Grade 5	$360.00		$
* Spanish Class set of 30 Grade 6	$360.00		$
* Teacher Edition must be ordered.		Subtotal	$

Teacher materials in English with critical thinking questions in English and Spanish.
All student blackline masters in Spanish.

For shipping charges add 10% of total order; $5.00 minimum charge $ _____

TOTAL $ _____

** Available June 2004

Bill McKinney, Ph.D., Executive Director
Region IV ESC is an equal opportunity employer